THE DATA WHISPERER -See the Patterns. Break the Loop. Reclaim Your Life

THE DATA WHISPERER -See the Patterns. Break the Loop. Reclaim Your Life

Kala Montena

1

The Data Whisperer

See the Patterns. Break the Loop. Reclaim Your Life

By **Kala Montena**

"In the space between human intuition and machine intelligence lies the future of consciousness itself."

Evolution of Consciousness in the Digital Age

"In the beginning was the Word, and the Word was with God, and the Word was God. All things were made through Him, and without Him nothing was made that was made. In Him was life, and the life was the light of men." - John 1:1-4

"The Tao that can be spoken is not the eternal Tao. The name that can be named is not the eternal name. The nameless is the beginning of heaven and earth. The named is the mother of ten thousand things." - Laozi, Tao Te Ching

"What we observe is not nature itself, but nature exposed to our method of questioning." - Werner Heisenberg

"We are not going to be able to operate our Spaceship Earth successfully nor for much longer unless we see it as a whole spaceship and our fate as common." - Buckminster Fuller

"The future is not some place we are going to, but one we are creating. The paths are not to be found, but made, and the activity of making them changes both the maker and the destination." - John Schaar

Welcome to Your Data Journey

Every morning, you wake up to an alarm set by an algorithm that learned your sleep patterns. You check your phone and see notifications curated by artificial intelligence that knows your interests better than some of your friends do. You drive to work using GPS that calculates the fastest route based on real-time traffic data from millions of other drivers. At lunch, you get restaurant recommendations from an app that has analyzed your dining history, location, and the preferences of people similar to you.

By the time you go to bed, you've interacted with dozens of algorithms, generated thousands of data points, and made countless decisions influenced by data you never saw. You live in a world where data shapes everything from the news you read to the products you buy, from the job opportunities you see to the people you meet on dating apps.

Yet most of us navigate this data-driven world with about as much understanding as our ancestors had of electricity when they first flipped a light switch. We know it works, we depend on it completely, but we have little idea how it actually functions or how to make it work better for us.

This book is your guide to changing that.

Why You Need This Book Now

We're living through the most dramatic transformation in how information works since the invention of writing. Every day, we create 2.5 quintillion bytes of data—that's 2.5 followed by 18 zeros. To put that in perspective, 90% of all the data in the world has been created in just the last two years.

This isn't just a technology story. It's a human story about power, privacy, opportunity, and choice. The companies and individuals who understand how to work with data are gaining unprecedented advantages, while those who don't are increasingly left behind. The gap between the data-literate and the data-illiterate is becoming one of the most important divides in our society.

But here's the good news: you don't need a computer science degree to become data-literate. You don't need to learn programming or statistics. You just need to understand how data works in your daily life and develop some practical skills for working with it more effectively.

What Makes This Book Different

Most books about data are written by experts for experts. They're full of technical jargon, complex formulas, and abstract concepts that feel disconnected from real life. This book is different. It's written for regular people who want practical knowledge they can use immediately.

You'll learn through stories, examples, and hands-on exercises that relate directly to your daily experience. Instead of abstract theories about machine learning, you'll discover how Netflix decides what to recommend and how you can train it to give you better suggestions. Instead of statistical formulas, you'll learn how to spot misleading claims in news articles and advertisements. Instead of privacy policy legalese, you'll get step-by-step guides for actually protecting your personal information.

Every chapter includes practical exercises you can do right away, tools you can start using today, and real-world applications that will make an immediate difference in your life. By the time you finish this book, you'll have developed what I call "data intuition"—the ability to quickly assess data claims, understand how algorithms affect you, and make better decisions using the information available to you.

Your Data Transformation Journey

Think of this book as a journey from data overwhelm to data empowerment. Right now, you might feel like data is something that happens to you—algorithms make decisions about what you see, companies collect your information without your understanding, and you're constantly bombarded with statistics and claims you can't evaluate.

By the end of this journey, you'll feel like data is something you can work with actively and confidently. You'll understand how to protect your privacy without giving up the benefits of digital services. You'll know how to find reliable information and spot manipulation. You'll be able to use data to make better decisions about everything from your health to your finances to your career.

Most importantly, you'll develop the confidence that comes from understanding how the systems around you actually work. Instead of feeling like a passive victim of algorithmic manipulation, you'll become an active participant who can shape your digital experience.

How to Use This Book

This book is designed to be both a complete journey and a practical reference. You can read it straight through for a comprehensive education in data literacy, or you can jump to specific chapters that address your immediate needs.

Each chapter builds on previous concepts, but I've also made sure that each one can stand alone.

Throughout the book, you'll find three types of practical elements:

Quick Wins are simple actions you can take immediately to improve your data situation. These might be privacy settings to change, tools to download, or habits to develop.

Deep Dives are more comprehensive exercises that will significantly enhance your data literacy. These might involve auditing your digital footprint, analyzing your personal data, or conducting research projects.

Real-World Applications are stories and case studies that show how the concepts apply to actual situations you might encounter.

A Personal Note

I want to be upfront about something: I'm not anti-technology or anti-data. I believe that data and algorithms can make our lives better in countless ways. They help us discover new music, find our way in unfamiliar cities, connect with people who share our interests, and solve problems we couldn't tackle before.

But I also believe that these powerful tools work best when we understand them and can make informed choices about how to use them. The goal isn't to avoid data or algorithms—that's impossible in the modern world. The goal is to develop the knowledge and skills to work with them consciously and effectively.

This book will help you become what I call a "data whisperer"—someone who can understand the language of data, communicate effectively with algorithmic systems, and use information strategically to achieve your goals. You'll learn to work with data rather than being worked over by it.

What You'll Gain

By the time you finish this book, you'll have developed several crucial capabilities:

Data Awareness: You'll understand how data flows through your daily life and recognize when you're creating, consuming, or being influenced by data.

Critical Evaluation: You'll know how to assess the reliability and relevance of data claims, whether they come from news articles, advertisements, or research studies.

Privacy Protection: You'll have practical skills for protecting your personal information while still enjoying the benefits of digital services.

Smart Consumption: You'll know how to use data to make better decisions about purchases, investments, health choices, and other important life decisions.

Algorithm Literacy: You'll understand how algorithmic systems work and how to interact with them more effectively.

Information Management: You'll have strategies for dealing with information overload and finding reliable sources in a noisy digital environment.

Future Readiness: You'll be prepared for emerging technologies like artificial intelligence and know how to adapt as the data landscape continues to evolve.

Your Journey Starts Now

The world of data can seem overwhelming, but remember that every expert started as a beginner. The most important step is simply beginning to pay attention to how data works in your life. Once you start noticing the patterns, everything else becomes much easier.

You don't need to become a data scientist or a privacy expert overnight. You just need to become a more conscious and capable participant in the data-driven world around you. This book will show you how to do that, one practical step at a time.

Welcome to your data journey. **Let's begin.**

DEDICATION

To the mother in Nairobi who wonders why her daughter no longer looks her in the eye.

To the student in São Paulo who can't focus, can't sleep, and thinks it's his fault.

To the father in Mumbai who works two jobs and still feels behind.

To the teenager in Seoul who compares her life to a feed and always comes up short.

To the grandmother in Mississippi who sees the world changing faster than anyone explains.

To the monk in Bhutan who never touched a phone but still prays for those of us who do.

To the child born today—

May you grow up in a world where your worth is not determined by an algorithm.

This book is for you.

And for all of us waking up inside the machine.

A NOTE TO THE READER

You don't need to understand computers to read this book.

You don't need to know how artificial intelligence works.

You just need to be human.

If you've ever opened your phone and felt more drained than inspired...

If you've ever caught yourself scrolling for no reason...

If you've ever felt like you were losing time, losing clarity, or losing yourself—

You are not alone.

This is not a book about technology.

It's a book about you.

A book about how the world we live in is quietly, constantly being shaped—

not by brute force, but by suggestion.

Not by law, but by code.

Not by conspiracy, but by design.

You will not find fear-mongering here.

You will not find false promises.

What you will find is a mirror.

And, if you're willing to look closely, a way home to yourself.

INTRODUCTION

You Are Not Broken. You Are Being Programmed.

There is a quiet crisis spreading across the world.

It doesn't always make headlines.

It doesn't look like disaster.

In fact, it often looks like convenience.

We wake up to glowing screens.

We reach for our phones before we breathe.

We scroll through images of lives not our own.

We compare, consume, repeat.

We feel exhausted by choices we don't remember making.

We question our attention spans, our willpower, our worth.

We whisper things to ourselves like,

"I should be more productive."

"I should be more grateful."

"I should be more like them."

But here's the truth—

You are not lazy.

You are not weak.

You are not broken.

You are responding—perfectly—to a world that was designed to extract your attention, shape your identity, and sell it back to you.

This is the age of the algorithmic self.

In every corner of the world—from Lagos to London, from Jakarta to Haiti—people are beginning to sense that something has changed. Not just in what we do, but in who we are. In how we think. In what we believe. In what we become.

We've always been shaped by our environments.

But now our environments are being shaped by code.

That code decides what news you see.

What products you're shown.

What job you might get.

Who you date.

What you believe.

And it's doing all this not by force—But by watching.

Learning.

Optimizing.

Not for your well-being.

But for your engagement.

For your time.

For your data.

So what does this mean for us—humans with hearts and histories, with culture and soul?

It means we are being shaped in ways we don't fully see.

It means we must learn to see again.

Not just to understand the systems we're inside,

but to understand ourselves—and to remember what it means to be human in an age that often forgets.

This book is a map.

It will take you through the hidden architecture of your digital life.

It will show you how your identity is being shaped,
how your attention is being steered,
and how your choices are being framed.
But more than that, it will offer you tools.
Real, practical, grounded steps to take back your time, your mind, your presence, your power.
We will move across borders and disciplines:
from behavioral psychology to ancient myth,
from neuroscience to indigenous wisdom,
from machine learning to moral philosophy.
You'll meet real people—across cultures, generations, and geographies—
who are living through the same questions you are.
And together, we'll ask:

- How do we stay grounded in a world that wants us addicted?
- How do we stay awake in a system built to distract us?
- How do we protect our children from forces even we don't fully understand?
- How do we build lives that feel true—when everything around us is constantly shifting?

You won't find all the answers here.
But you will find something more important:
A compass.
A challenge.
And a return.
Because underneath all the code,
beyond the screens,
there is still you.
And you were never meant to be optimized.
You were meant to be free.

Foreword

Every so often, a book emerges that doesn't merely describe the world—it transforms how you engage with it. *The Data Whisperer* is one of those rare works.

In an age where every action, interaction, and decision leaves a digital footprint, we are surrounded by whispers—subtle patterns that quietly shape our lives. These whispers influence our choices, habits, relationships, and futures, carrying the potential to empower or confine us. Yet, for many, the world of data feels distant and overwhelming—a labyrinth of numbers and algorithms seemingly reserved for the experts.

This book changes that. *The Data Whisperer* is not just a guide to understanding data; it is an invitation to see your life and the world through a sharper, more meaningful lens. By revealing the invisible threads that connect our decisions, relationships, and aspirations, this book bridges the gap between complexity and clarity. It transforms data from an abstract concept into a practical, transformative force—accessible to anyone, regardless of background or expertise.

Through engaging stories, actionable insights, and thought-provoking ethical considerations, this book goes far beyond statistics. It explores how data shapes not only what we do but who we are, who we have the potential to become, and the kind of world we can create together. With every chapter, *The Data Whisperer* empowers you to move from being a passive observer of information to an active architect of your destiny.

Whether you are a seasoned professional, a curious learner, or someone simply seeking a deeper understanding of the patterns that define our existence, this book is for you. It is a guide to personal empowerment and collective transformation in the age of information—a call to listen, to understand, and to lead.

The whispers are all around us, waiting to be heard. Are you ready to tune in and harness their power?

—Kala Montena

Unlocking Hidden Patterns That Shape Our World

The Whisper That Shapes Your World

The fluorescent lights buzzed softly as the father stormed into his local Target. Clutching a stack of advertisements, his anger filled the air before he even spoke.

"What are you trying to pull?" he demanded, his voice sharp and accusatory. "Are you encouraging my daughter to get pregnant?"

The manager froze, his apology quick but uncertain. The offending advertisements—featuring cribs, diapers, and baby clothes—lay sprawled across the counter like evidence in a case yet to be made. "My daughter is still in high school!" the father continued, his voice rising with each word.

The tension was palpable as the father left, slamming the door behind him. Days passed.

When the man returned, his demeanor was entirely different. His shoulders slumped, his voice quieter now.

"I owe you an apology," he began, eyes fixed on the floor. "It turns out my daughter is pregnant. I didn't know."

This story, later chronicled in news outlets worldwide, revealed a startling truth: Target's algorithms had predicted the daughter's pregnancy before her own family did. By analyzing subtle patterns in purchasing behavior—like unscented lotion and vitamin supplements—the company had uncovered a reality invisible to the naked eye.

This is the extraordinary power of data: it connects dots we don't even know exist, revealing patterns that shape decisions, predict behaviors, and sometimes uncover secrets we aren't ready to face. These patterns—these whispers in the data—are all around us. They are the invisible threads weaving through our lives, shaping our choices and influencing our futures.

Patterns Beneath the Surface

Every choice you make leaves a trail of data. Each click, swipe, and purchase contributes to an intricate web of information. In 2025, the world is projected to generate over **175 zettabytes of data annually**—enough to fill over 2 billion 1-terabyte hard drives every year. Within this flood of information lie insights that have the power to transform our understanding of the world and ourselves.

Consider this: studies show that **93% of human communication is non-verbal**—a statistic that underscores how much of what we convey lies beneath the surface. Similarly, data reveals truths that are often hidden, even from our conscious awareness. For example, researchers have found that online search trends can predict flu outbreaks up to **two weeks before official reports**, simply by analyzing search terms like "flu symptoms" and "cold remedies."

These patterns aren't just abstract. They're actionable. They reveal how small, seemingly inconsequential choices ripple outward, shaping outcomes in ways we often overlook.

The Power and Responsibility of Patterns

Imagine walking through a city at night. To the untrained eye, it's a chaotic sprawl of lights, sounds, and motion. But to someone who understands how to look, it's a symphony of patterns: the ebb and flow of traffic, the clustering of pedestrians, the rhythm of streetlights guiding the way.

Data operates in much the same way. It transforms chaos into clarity, revealing the invisible structures that govern our lives. But with this power comes a responsibility.

Algorithms can illuminate opportunities, but they can also perpetuate inequalities. Predictive insights can enhance our lives, but they can also invade our privacy. Consider that **80% of hiring decisions in Fortune 500 companies are now influenced by AI**. While this streamlines the process, it raises pressing ethical questions about bias and fairness.

Understanding patterns isn't just about unlocking potential—it's about navigating these complexities with wisdom and integrity.

Your Role in the Story

This book isn't just about data—it's about you. It's about equipping you with the tools to decode the patterns shaping your world, from the deeply personal to the profoundly societal.

Think about your daily habits: the apps you open first thing in the morning, the routes you take to work, the purchases you make without a second thought. These aren't random actions—they're data points in a larger story. Studies show that **45% of our daily actions are driven by habits**, which means nearly half of what we do operates on autopilot. What if you could rewrite those patterns? What if you could align them with your goals, transforming unconscious routines into deliberate actions?

Now scale that idea up. Consider the patterns that govern communities, organizations, even entire nations. From the spread of misinformation online to the adoption of sustainable energy practices, data offers us the power to influence these larger systems—if we know how to listen to it.

Table of Contents

CHAPTER 1

THE MIRROR THAT THINKS

How Algorithms Learn Who You Are — And Then Decide Who You Should Be

The Scroll

It begins with a flick of your thumb.
You're standing in a pharmacy line in Nairobi.
Swaying in a subway car in New York.
Lying awake at 3:04 a.m. in Tokyo.
You don't think. You just reach.
Scroll.

Pause.
Tap.
Swipe.
And in that instant—something wakes up.
Not a person. A system.
It watches:

- What holds your gaze a moment longer.
- What makes you tap without knowing why.
- What you skip, but not quite fast enough.

It doesn't see your heart.
But it memorizes your habit.
And then, like a mirror that has learned to whisper,
it begins speaking back.

The Illusion of Help

At first, it feels like magic.
Your music app knows your mood before you do.
Your food app guesses your craving.
Your streaming service finishes your sentence.
But it's not magic.
It's math.
And it's not predicting who you are.
It's predicting what you're likely to do next—
based on what you've already done.
This is the logic of the thinking mirror:
Reflect the past. Shape the future.
And with every helpful suggestion,
the world around you becomes a little smaller.
A little sharper.
A little more like you used to be.

A Broken Reflection

In ancient Morocco, mirrors were crafted from polished metal—
hand-forged, sacred objects used to reflect truth,
not appearance alone.
They were slow to make.
Heavy to carry.
And not to be looked into lightly.
Today, we face a new mirror.
Faster. Brighter. Endless.
But it reflects only what is:

- Measurable.
- Trackable.
- Profitable.

It doesn't see your questions—only your clicks.
Not your values—only your velocity.
Not your longing—only your pattern.
To the mirror:
If you hovered, you wanted it.
If you returned, you believed in it.
If you paused, you consented.
This mirror never asks:
"Is this who you want to be?"
It only answers:
"This is who you are."

The Cairo Experiment

A woman in Cairo watches a video about astrology.
She doesn't believe in it—she's just curious.
The system takes note:
She finished the video.
So the mirror responds:

Tarot cards.
Birth charts.
Cosmic predictions.
Within days, her digital world is dripping in stars and symbols.
She didn't ask for this.
She was nudged.
And slowly, she begins to interpret life through that lens.
Not because it's true.
But because it's all she sees.
This is how identity is shaped not by belief—
but by repetition.
Not by decision—
but by drift.
Not by truth—
but by exposure.

The Algorithm as Teacher

In the 1970s, psychologist Albert Bandura uncovered a truth as old as story itself:

We become what we observe.
Now imagine a teenage girl in Manila.
Her world is a screen.
Beauty filters soften her skin.
Perfect lives parade past her eyes.
Comments dissect her body with surgical cruelty.
She learns—not through words, but through frequency—
what is beautiful, what is desirable,
what is worth being.
The algorithm never says it out loud.
It simply shows the same thing
until it feels like reality.

The Business of You

This isn't evil.
It's efficient.
The system wasn't built to harm you.
It was built to keep you.
And what holds human attention best?

- Outrage.
- Fear.
- Desire.
- Novelty.
- Validation.

So the mirror feeds them to you.
Over and over.
Until they don't just capture you—
They become you.
Engage. React. Stay.
Stay. Scroll. Become.
This is not a conspiracy.
It's a business model.
And you are the product.

Breaking the Reflection

Can you choose differently?
Yes.
But not by accident.
It takes:

- Awareness — the ability to see the mirror
- Friction — the willingness to pause
- Defiance — the quiet courage to resist the default

Because if you don't disrupt the pattern,
the pattern will define you.
And you are not here to be defined.
You are here to remember.

Practice: Rewriting the Reflection

Try this:

1. Open a platform you use every day.
2. Scroll—slowly.
3. After 10 posts, stop.
4. Ask:
    - Is this me?
    - Or is this the mirror talking back?

Write what you notice.
Don't analyze. Just witness.
This is not about guilt.
It's about awakening.
This feed is not the world.
This mirror is not your mind.
And you are more than a pattern waiting to be predicted.

AWAKENING TO DATA

Understanding the invisible forces shaping your world

Data Is Everywhere (And It's Watching You)

Sarah thought she was having a private moment. She was sitting in her car in the parking lot of a medical clinic, taking a few minutes to process some difficult news she'd just received. She wasn't on her phone, wasn't posting on social media, wasn't even listening to music. She was just sitting quietly, thinking.

What Sarah didn't realize was that her car was recording her location and storing it in a database that would later be sold to data brokers. Her phone was logging which cell towers it connected to and how long she stayed in each location. The clinic's WiFi network had automatically logged her device's unique identifier. Her credit card company had recorded the payment for her appointment. Her health insurance app had noted that she'd visited a medical facility.

Even in what felt like a completely private moment, Sarah was generating data that would be collected, analyzed, and used to make decisions about her life.

Within weeks, she would start seeing targeted advertisements for medical services. Her insurance company would use location data to verify her claims. Marketing companies would add her to lists of people who visit certain types of medical facilities.

Sarah's story isn't unusual—it's the reality for all of us, every day. We live in a world where data collection has become so pervasive and sophisticated that we're constantly generating information about ourselves, often without realizing it. Understanding this reality is the first step toward taking control of your data life.

Your Morning Data Trail

Let's trace a typical morning to see just how much data you create before you even leave for work. This exercise will help you develop what I call "data awareness"—the ability to recognize when you're creating, consuming, or being influenced by data.

You wake up to an alarm on your smartphone. Immediately, several data points are created: what time you woke up, how many times you hit snooze, how long you slept, and possibly even data about your sleep quality if you use a sleep tracking app. Your phone's accelerometer and gyroscope have been monitoring your movements all night, creating a detailed record of your sleep patterns.

You check your phone for messages and notifications. Each app you open logs your usage: what time you opened it, how long you spent in it, what content you viewed, and what actions you took. Your email app notes which messages you opened, how long you spent reading them, and whether you replied. Your social media apps record which posts you viewed, how long you looked at each one, and whether you liked, shared, or commented.

You ask your smart speaker for the weather forecast. This creates multiple data points: your voice pattern (which can be used to identify you), the time of your request, your location (inferred from your IP address), and your interest in weather information. The device also records background noise, which can reveal information about your household size, pets, and daily routines.

You start your car and use GPS navigation to check traffic conditions. Your car's computer logs when you started the engine, your starting location, your destination, your route, your speed, and your driving patterns. The GPS app on your phone creates a detailed record of your journey, including stops, delays, and alternative routes considered.

You stop at a coffee shop and pay with your credit card or mobile payment app. This creates a record of your location, the time of purchase, the amount spent, and the specific items bought. If you use a loyalty card or app, even more detailed information is collected about your preferences and purchasing patterns.

By the time you arrive at work, you've already generated hundreds of data points that paint a detailed picture of your morning routine, your preferences, your location patterns, and your behavior. And this is just the beginning of your day.

The Invisible Web of Data Collection

What makes modern data collection so powerful—and so concerning—is that it's largely invisible. Unlike traditional forms of surveillance, which required obvious cameras or recording devices, digital data collection happens silently in the background of our daily activities.

Consider your smartphone, which is essentially a sophisticated surveillance device that you carry with you everywhere. It contains multiple sensors that can track your location, movement, orientation, and even your health metrics. It has microphones that can record audio, cameras that can capture images and video, and network connections that can transmit all of this information in real-time.

But your phone is just one part of a vast ecosystem of data collection. Your smart TV monitors what you watch and when. Your fitness tracker records your physical activity, heart rate, and sleep patterns. Your smart home devices listen for voice commands and monitor your daily routines. Your car tracks your driving habits and locations. Your credit cards record every purchase you make.

Even when you're not actively using technology, you're still generating data. Security cameras with facial recognition technology can identify you as you walk down the street. License plate readers can track your car's movements. Bluetooth beacons in stores can detect when your phone enters their vicinity. WiFi networks can log your device's unique identifier even if you don't connect to them.

This web of data collection is coordinated by an industry most people have never heard of: data brokers. These companies specialize in collecting, aggregating, and selling personal information. They purchase data from thousands of sources—apps, websites, retailers, government records, and more—and combine it to create detailed profiles of individuals.

The result is that companies you've never heard of may know more about your daily habits, preferences, and behavior than your closest friends and family members do. They know where you live and work, what you buy, where you travel, what websites you visit, what apps you use, and much more.

Why This Matters Now More Than Ever

You might be thinking, "So what? I'm not doing anything wrong, and if companies want to show me more relevant ads, that seems fine." This reaction is understandable, but it misses the bigger picture of how data collection affects your life in ways that go far beyond advertising.

First, the data collected about you is used to make important decisions that affect your opportunities and outcomes. Insurance companies use data to set your premiums and decide whether to cover you. Employers use data to screen job candidates. Landlords use data to evaluate rental applications. Banks use data to determine your creditworthiness. Dating apps use data to decide who you see and who sees you.

These algorithmic decisions can create or limit opportunities in ways that are often invisible to you. You might never know that you didn't get a job interview because an algorithm flagged something in your digital profile, or that you're paying higher insurance premiums because of data about your neighborhood or shopping habits.

Second, the constant collection and analysis of personal data is changing how companies and institutions relate to individuals. Instead of treating you as a customer or citizen with rights and agency, they increasingly treat you as a collection of data points to be analyzed and influenced. This shift has profound implications for autonomy, privacy, and human dignity.

Third, the concentration of data in the hands of a few large technology companies is creating unprecedented imbalances of power. These companies know more about individuals and society than any institution in human history, and they use this knowledge to influence behavior, shape markets, and affect political outcomes.

Finally, the current system of data collection is largely unregulated and operates without meaningful consent from the people whose data is being collected. Most privacy policies are deliberately confusing and designed to obscure rather than explain what's actually happening with your information.

The Cost of Data Ignorance

To understand why data literacy matters, let's look at some real-world examples of what can happen when people don't understand how their data is being collected and used.

The Location Tracking Scandal: In 2018, it was revealed that Google had been tracking the location of Android users even when they had turned off location services. The company was collecting location data through other means, including WiFi and cellular tower connections. Users who thought they had opted out of location tracking discovered that Google had detailed records of their movements going back years.

The Credit Score Surprise: Maria, a teacher from Phoenix, discovered that her credit score had dropped significantly, affecting her ability to refinance her mortgage. After investigating, she found that a data broker had incorrectly associated her with someone else who had the same name and lived in the same city. The incorrect information had been sold to credit reporting agencies, and it took months of effort to correct the error.

The Insurance Investigation: John, a small business owner, was surprised when his health insurance company questioned a claim for a routine medical procedure. The company had purchased location data showing that John frequently visited a medical facility that specialized in treating a chronic condition he had never disclosed. The insurance company used this information to investigate whether John had failed to disclose a pre-existing condition when he applied for coverage.

The Job Search Mystery: Lisa couldn't understand why she wasn't getting responses to her job applications despite being well-qualified for the positions. She later discovered that an automated screening system was filtering out her applications because an algorithm had determined that people from her zip code were less likely to be successful in certain types of roles.

The Price Discrimination Discovery: David noticed that he was seeing higher prices for the same products when shopping online compared to his friends. Investigation revealed that the retailer was using data about his browsing history, location, and device type to determine that he was likely to pay higher prices, and was showing him inflated costs accordingly.

These examples illustrate how data collection and algorithmic decision-making can affect your life in concrete, material ways. The people in these stories weren't doing anything wrong—they were simply unaware of how their data was being collected and used against their interests.

Taking Back Control: Your Data Empowerment Journey

The goal of this book isn't to make you paranoid about data collection or to convince you to abandon digital technology. That would be neither practical nor desirable in the modern world. Instead, the goal is to help you become a more informed and empowered participant in the data ecosystem.

Think of it like learning to drive. When you first get behind the wheel of a car, the experience can be overwhelming. There are so many things to pay attention to: the road, other drivers, traffic signals, your speed, your fuel level, and more. But with practice and knowledge, driving becomes second nature. You develop the skills and awareness to navigate safely and efficiently.

Data literacy works the same way. Right now, navigating the data-driven world might feel overwhelming because there's so much happening that you can't see or understand. But with the right knowledge and skills, you can learn to work with data systems confidently and effectively.

The first step is developing data awareness—learning to recognize when you're creating, consuming, or being influenced by data. This chapter has started that process by helping you see the data trail you create in your daily activities. As you continue through this book, you'll develop more sophisticated skills for understanding and working with data.

You'll learn how algorithms make decisions and how you can influence those decisions to get better outcomes. You'll discover how to protect your privacy without giving up the benefits of digital services. You'll develop the ability to evaluate data claims critically and spot manipulation. You'll gain practical skills for using data to make better decisions in your own life.

Most importantly, you'll develop confidence. Instead of feeling like a passive victim of algorithmic systems, you'll become an active participant who understands how these systems work and how to make them work better for you.

Quick Wins: Immediate Steps to Increase Data Awareness

Before we dive deeper into how data systems work, here are some simple actions you can take right now to start developing data awareness and taking more control over your digital life:

Conduct a Data Diary Exercise: For one full day, keep a record of every time you interact with a digital device or service. Note when you use your phone, what apps you open, when you make purchases, when you use GPS, and any other digital interactions. This will help you visualize the scope of your data creation.

Review Your App Permissions: Go through the apps on your phone and review what permissions you've granted them. Many apps request access to your location, contacts, camera, microphone, and other sensitive information. Revoke permissions that aren't necessary for the app's core function.

Check Your Google Activity: If you use Google services, visit myactivity.google.com to see what the company has recorded about your searches, location history, YouTube viewing, and other activities. This will give you a concrete sense of how much data one company can collect about you.

Examine Your Social Media Data: Most social media platforms allow you to download a copy of your data. Request this data from Facebook, Twitter, Instagram, or other platforms you use. You'll be surprised by how much information they have about you, including data you never explicitly provided.

Audit Your Email Subscriptions: Look through your email inbox and unsubscribe from newsletters and promotional emails you don't actually want. Each of these subscriptions represents a data relationship where companies are tracking your engagement and building profiles of your interests.

These exercises will give you a concrete sense of your current data footprint and help you start thinking more consciously about your digital interactions. They're also the foundation for more advanced data literacy skills you'll develop in the coming chapters.

Understanding that data is everywhere and constantly watching you might feel overwhelming at first. That's a normal reaction to realizing the scope of modern data collection. But remember that awareness is the first step toward empowerment.

As we continue through this book, you'll develop increasingly sophisticated skills for navigating the data-driven world. You'll learn to protect what needs protecting, optimize what can be optimized, and use data as a tool for making better decisions in your own life.

The goal isn't to become a data expert overnight. It's to become a more conscious and capable participant in the digital world around you. Every small step you take toward understanding how data works in your life is a step toward greater autonomy and empowerment.

What Comes Next

In the next chapter, we move deeper.
Not into the feed—
but into the self.
What happens when every choice is tailored?
When identity is curated more than cultivated?
Who are you when the mirror whispers louder than your own voice?
Because once a reflection learns to think...
it begins to shape.
And if you're not careful,
it starts to decide.

Your data journey has ***begun***. Let's continue exploring this fascinating and important landscape together.

CHAPTER 2

THE RISE OF THE ALGORITHMIC SELF

Why You're Not Crazy—You're Being Pulled in Ten Directions at Once

A man sits on a rooftop in Istanbul.

The call to prayer echoes in the background.

He checks his phone, just for a moment.

By the time he looks up again, it's dark.

He doesn't remember what he saw—only that it never felt like enough.

A teenager in Lagos refreshes her feed.

She sees a protest, a dance trend, a war, a lipstick tutorial, a suicide hotline, a meme.

She closes the app with a headache.

Not because the world is too big—

But because her self feels too small.

Across continents, this quiet question rises:

Who am I becoming—when everything I see is designed for someone I used to be?

The Personal Becomes Programmable

We are living through a shift so deep it's hard to name.

We are no longer just individuals with preferences.

We are profiles.

Data doubles.

Behavioral signatures.

The way you tap, the angle you hold your phone, the speed of your reply—

These are no longer invisible.

They are inputs.

And those inputs build a version of you.

A simplified one.

A version that can be predicted, targeted, monetized.

This version is not your soul.

It's your statistical shadow.

And the systems that surround you increasingly serve this shadow—

Not your fullness. Not your mystery. Not your becoming.

When Everything Is Tailored, Nothing Feels True

You watch a video on grief.
Now your feed becomes a therapy couch.
You buy a book on parenting.
Now every ad assumes you're a mother.
You click on a story about war.
Now your homepage becomes a battlefield.
The world begins to curve around your past clicks—
as if that is who you are, who you want to be, what you want to see.
And even when you try to break free,
the system pulls you back with a whisper:
"We thought you'd like this."
It's not malicious. It's mechanical.
But the result is emotional:
Disorientation. Identity fatigue. Inner fragmentation.

The Shattered Mirror

In many cultures, the soul is thought to be singular but complex—
A harmony of parts: thinker, feeler, dreamer, doer.
In Zulu philosophy, there is the concept of ubuntu—
A person is a person through other people.
Identity is collective, lived through connection.
But algorithms do not honor complexity.
They slice us into pieces.
Your music app knows your joy.
Your news app knows your rage.
Your fitness tracker knows your shame.
Your camera roll holds your secret longings.
Your social feed knows your polished mask.
And none of them speak to each other.
So we walk through the world like a mosaic of selves,
each version curated for a different interface,
none of them whole.

The Loss of the Inner Compass

When every part of life is optimized—
for speed, for relevance, for convenience—
something sacred is lost:
Discernment.
The slow, steady practice of deciding for yourself.
We begin to mistake algorithmic suggestions for personal desires.
We forget how to ask:
Do I want this?
Or was it simply shown to me enough times?
And when we stop asking those questions,
we stop knowing who we are.

The Algorithmic Self Is Addictive Because It Feels Like Belonging

When you see your beliefs echoed back to you,
your preferences reflected,
your humor understood—
it feels like truth. Like home. Like self.
But is it?
Or is it a hall of mirrors?
A trap made of familiarity?
A loop of reinforcement?
And if you step outside of it—
into silence, into boredom, into contradiction—
Do you still know how to recognize yourself?

A Global Pattern, A Human Cost

In Seoul, a college student deletes all her apps and still feels the ghost of the scroll.

In Johannesburg, a teacher tries to reconnect with his students beyond the screens.

In Paris, a mother watches her son spend more time with code than with people.

In Manila, an elder tells a child a story—with no algorithm between them.

All around the world, the question hums beneath the surface:

What does it mean to be human in a system that never stops suggesting who you should be?

You Are Not the Problem

If you feel scattered, overwhelmed, disconnected—

That's not a personal failure.

That's a rational response to a world optimized for fragmentation.

You were not designed to be constantly updated.

You were not built to process a thousand opinions before coffee.

You were not meant to compare your life to a highlight reel curated by machines.

You were meant to live from the inside out.

Not from the outside in.

And it is still possible.

The Practice: Digital Self-Inquiry

This week, choose one digital space you use daily.

Instagram. YouTube. TikTok. LinkedIn. Spotify.

- Ask: What version of me is this space reinforcing?
- Is that version aligned with who I am—or just who I've been?

Then try this:

- Post or engage in a way that reflects a different part of you—something not usually shared.
- Notice how the platform responds.
- More importantly, notice how you feel.

The goal is not to escape the system—
but to interrupt the automation of your identity.
To remind yourself that you are not a brand.
You are not a persona.
You are a person.
And that is enough.

Algorithms: The Invisible Decision Makers

Marcus couldn't figure out why his job search was going so poorly. He had solid experience, good references, and was applying for positions that seemed like perfect matches for his background. Yet after months of applications, he was getting very few interviews and no job offers.

What Marcus didn't know was that most of his applications were being filtered out before any human ever saw them. The companies he was applying to used automated screening systems—algorithms—that analyzed resumes and ranked candidates based on various factors. These algorithms had learned patterns from past hiring decisions, and unfortunately, they had learned some problematic patterns too.

The algorithm noticed that Marcus had a gap in his employment history from when he took time off to care for his sick father. It flagged this as a negative indicator, even though the gap was clearly explained in his cover letter. The algorithm also noticed that Marcus lived in a zip code that the system had learned to associate with lower-performing employees, based on historical data that reflected past discrimination rather than actual job performance.

Marcus was being rejected not by human prejudice, but by algorithmic prejudice—bias that had been encoded into software and was now being applied at scale. He was experiencing firsthand how algorithms can make decisions that profoundly affect our lives, often in ways we never see or understand.

Understanding how algorithms work and how they affect you is crucial for navigating the modern world. These invisible decision-makers are everywhere, shaping what you see, what opportunities you get, and how you're treated by institutions and companies. Learning to work with them effectively is one of the most important skills you can develop.

What Is an Algorithm? (In Plain English)

Despite all the mystique surrounding them, algorithms are actually quite simple in concept. An algorithm is just a set of rules for making decisions or solving problems. It's a step-by-step process that takes some input, processes it according to predetermined rules, and produces an output.

Think of a recipe for baking cookies. The recipe tells you what ingredients to use (inputs), what steps to follow (processing rules), and what you should end up with (output). An algorithm works the same way, except instead of ingredients and cooking steps, it uses data and mathematical operations.

Here's a simple example of an algorithmic decision you might encounter: when you apply for a credit card, the bank uses an algorithm to decide whether to approve you. The algorithm takes inputs like your credit score, income, debt-to-income ratio, and employment history. It processes these inputs according to rules the bank has established (for example, "if credit score is above 700 and debt-to-income ratio is below 30%, approve"). Then it produces an output: approved or denied.

What makes modern algorithms powerful and sometimes problematic is that they can process vast amounts of data and make decisions much faster than humans could. They can also identify patterns in data that humans might miss. But they can also perpetuate biases, make errors, and optimize for goals that don't align with human values.

The algorithms that affect your daily life range from simple rule-based systems to sophisticated artificial intelligence that can learn and adapt. Understanding the different types will help you recognize how they work and how to interact with them more effectively.

The Algorithm Zoo: Types You Encounter Daily

Recommendation Algorithms are probably the algorithms you interact with most frequently. These systems analyze your past behavior to predict what you might want to see, buy, or do next. Netflix uses recommendation algorithms to suggest movies and TV shows. Amazon uses them to recommend products. Spotify uses them to create personalized playlists. Social media platforms use them to decide what posts to show you.

These algorithms work by finding patterns in your behavior and comparing you to other users with similar patterns. If you and another user both liked the same five movies, the algorithm might recommend movies that the other user liked but you haven't seen yet. The more data the algorithm has about your preferences, the better its recommendations can become.

Search Algorithms determine what results you see when you search for information online. Google's search algorithm considers hundreds of factors to decide which web pages to show you and in what order. These factors include the relevance of the content to your search terms, the authority and trustworthiness of the website, your location, your search history, and many other signals.

Understanding how search algorithms work can help you find better information more quickly. For example, knowing that Google personalizes results based on your location and search history can help you understand why you and a friend might see different results for the same search query.

Filtering Algorithms decide what content you see and don't see on social media platforms. Facebook, Twitter, Instagram, and other platforms use algorithms to filter through the thousands of potential posts you could see and show you the ones the algorithm thinks you're most likely to engage with.

These algorithms consider factors like your relationship to the person posting, how much you've interacted with their content in the past, how much other people are engaging with the post, and what type of content you typically engage with. The goal is to show you content that will keep you on the platform longer.

Pricing Algorithms are used by many companies to set prices dynamically based on various factors. Airlines use algorithms to adjust ticket prices based on demand, time until departure, and your browsing history. Ride-sharing apps use surge pricing algorithms to increase prices during high-demand periods. Some online retailers use algorithms to show different prices to different customers based on their perceived willingness to pay.

Matching Algorithms are used by platforms that connect people or match supply with demand. Dating apps use algorithms to decide which profiles to show you. Job platforms use algorithms to match job seekers with opportunities. Gig economy platforms use algorithms to match drivers with riders or workers with tasks.

Credit Scoring Algorithms analyze your financial history and behavior to predict how likely you are to repay loans. These algorithms consider factors like your payment history, the amount of debt you have, the length of your credit history, and the types of credit you use. Your credit score affects your ability to get loans, credit cards, mortgages, and sometimes even jobs and housing.

Fraud Detection Algorithms monitor your financial transactions and online activities to identify potentially fraudulent behavior. These algorithms look for patterns that deviate from your normal behavior, such as purchases in unusual locations or at unusual times. While these algorithms help protect you from fraud, they can sometimes flag legitimate activities as suspicious.

How Algorithms Learn About You: The Feedback Loop

One of the most important things to understand about modern algorithms is that many of them are designed to learn and improve over time. They do this through a process called machine learning, where the algorithm analyzes data to identify patterns and make predictions.

Here's how this learning process typically works in the context of a recommendation algorithm:

Initial Data Collection: The algorithm starts by collecting data about your behavior. This might include what products you view, what you purchase, how long you spend looking at different items, what you search for, and what you click on.

Pattern Recognition: The algorithm analyzes this data to identify patterns. It might notice that you tend to buy organic food products, that you're interested in science fiction books, or that you typically shop for clothes on weekends.

Prediction Making: Based on these patterns, the algorithm makes predictions about what you might be interested in. It might predict that you would like a new organic snack product or a recently released science fiction novel.

Recommendation Delivery: The algorithm shows you recommendations based on its predictions. You might see ads for organic products or suggestions for science fiction books.

Feedback Collection: The algorithm monitors how you respond to its recommendations. Do you click on them? Do you make purchases? Do you ignore them? This response data becomes new input for the algorithm.

Learning and Adjustment: Based on your feedback, the algorithm adjusts its understanding of your preferences and improves its future predictions. If you consistently ignore recommendations for science fiction books, the algorithm will learn that it was wrong about that interest and adjust accordingly.

This feedback loop means that algorithms are constantly evolving their understanding of you based on your behavior. The more you interact with algorithmic systems, the more data they have to work with, and the more accurate their predictions can become.

However, this learning process can also create problems. If an algorithm makes an incorrect assumption about you early on, your subsequent behavior might reinforce that assumption even if it's wrong. For example, if a job search algorithm incorrectly categorizes you as unqualified for certain types of positions, you might stop seeing those opportunities, which means you can't apply for them, which reinforces the algorithm's belief that you're not interested in or qualified for those roles.

When Algorithms Get It Wrong: Bias and Errors

Algorithms are often presented as objective and neutral, but they're actually full of human biases and assumptions. These biases can come from several sources:

Historical Bias: Many algorithms are trained on historical data that reflects past discrimination and inequality. If an algorithm learns from data showing that certain groups were historically excluded from opportunities, it might perpetuate that exclusion even when the original reasons for it are no longer valid or legal.

Representation Bias: Algorithms work best when they have lots of data to learn from. If certain groups are underrepresented in the training data, the algorithm might not work as well for those groups. For example, facial recognition systems have historically been less accurate for people with darker skin because they were primarily trained on images of lighter-skinned people.

Measurement Bias: Algorithms can only work with data that can be measured and quantified. This means they might miss important factors that are difficult to measure, or they might overemphasize factors that are easy to measure but not actually important.

Feedback Bias: The feedback loop that helps algorithms learn can also perpetuate bias. If an algorithm makes biased decisions and those decisions affect people's opportunities, the resulting data might make the bias appear justified even when it's not.

Design Bias: The people who design algorithms make choices about what factors to consider, how to weight different inputs, and what outcomes to optimize for. These choices reflect the designers' assumptions and priorities, which might not align with the needs and values of the people affected by the algorithm.

Understanding these sources of bias can help you recognize when algorithmic decisions might be unfair or inaccurate. It can also help you understand why you might be seeing certain recommendations or experiencing certain outcomes from algorithmic systems.

Real-World Algorithm Impacts

To understand how algorithms affect real people's lives, let's look at some specific examples:

Healthcare Algorithms: Hospitals use algorithms to help prioritize patient care and allocate resources. One widely used algorithm was found to systematically underestimate the healthcare needs of Black patients because it used healthcare spending as a proxy for health needs. Since Black patients historically had less access to healthcare and therefore lower spending, the algorithm incorrectly concluded they were healthier than they actually were.

Criminal Justice Algorithms: Courts use algorithms to help make decisions about bail, sentencing, and parole. These algorithms are supposed to predict the likelihood that someone will commit another crime. However, investigations have found that these algorithms often exhibit racial bias, incorrectly flagging Black defendants as higher risk than white defendants with similar backgrounds.

Hiring Algorithms: Many companies use algorithms to screen job applications and identify promising candidates. Amazon famously had to scrap a hiring algorithm because it was biased against women. The algorithm had learned from historical hiring data that showed men were more likely to be hired for technical roles, and it began penalizing resumes that included words associated with women.

Housing Algorithms: Landlords and property management companies increasingly use algorithms to screen rental applications. These algorithms might consider factors like credit scores, income, and employment history, but they can also perpetuate housing discrimination by using proxies for protected characteristics like race or family status.

Insurance Algorithms: Insurance companies use algorithms to set premiums and determine coverage. While this can help them price risk more accurately, it can also lead to discrimination. For example, some algorithms use social media data or shopping patterns to make inferences about people's health or lifestyle, which might not be accurate or fair.

Taking Back Control: Working with Algorithms, Not Against Them

The goal isn't to avoid algorithms—that's impossible in the modern world. Instead, the goal is to understand how they work and learn to interact with them more effectively. Here are some strategies for working with algorithmic systems:

Understand the Feedback Loop: Remember that most algorithms learn from your behavior, so you can influence their decisions by being intentional about your actions. If you don't like the recommendations you're getting from Netflix, rate movies and shows to give the algorithm better data about your preferences. If you want to see different types of content on social media, engage more with the content you want to see and less with content you don't.

Diversify Your Inputs: Algorithms can create filter bubbles by showing you more of what you've already shown interest in. To counteract this, actively seek out diverse sources of information and different types of content. Follow people with different perspectives on social media. Search for information using different terms. Shop at different websites.

Question the Recommendations: Don't assume that algorithmic recommendations are always in your best interest. Companies design algorithms to optimize for their goals, which might not align with yours. A recommendation algorithm might suggest products that are profitable for the company rather than best for you. A social media algorithm might show you content that keeps you engaged rather than content that makes you happy or informed.

Audit Your Digital Footprint: Regularly review the data that algorithms have about you and correct any errors. Check your credit reports for inaccuracies. Review your Google activity and delete searches or activities that don't represent your actual interests. Update your preferences on platforms you use regularly.

Use Multiple Sources: Don't rely on a single algorithmic system for important decisions. If you're job searching, use multiple job platforms. If you're looking for information, consult multiple search engines and sources. If you're making a major purchase, compare recommendations from different platforms.

Understand Your Rights: Learn about your rights regarding algorithmic decision-making. In some jurisdictions, you have the right to know when algorithms are being used to make decisions about you, to understand how those algorithms work, and to challenge algorithmic decisions.

Practical Exercises: Algorithm Awareness

Here are some hands-on exercises to help you understand how algorithms work in your daily life:

Social Media Algorithm Audit: For one week, pay close attention to what content appears in your social media feeds. Notice patterns in what you're shown. Then, deliberately engage with different types of content—like posts from friends you don't usually interact with, or content on topics you don't usually engage with. Observe how your feed changes in response.

Search Result Comparison: Choose a topic you're interested in and search for it using different search engines (Google, Bing, DuckDuckGo). Compare the results you get. Then try the same search from different devices or locations, or after clearing your search history. Notice how the results differ.

Recommendation Reset: Pick a platform that gives you recommendations (Netflix, Spotify, Amazon, etc.) and deliberately interact with content outside your usual preferences. Like different types of movies, listen to different genres of music, or browse different categories of products. Observe how the recommendations change over time.

Price Comparison: When shopping online, compare prices for the same product across different websites and different devices. Try searching for the same item using different browsers or in incognito mode. Notice if you see different prices.

Algorithm Transparency Research: Look up the companies and platforms you use regularly and research what they've disclosed about how their algorithms work. Many companies publish blog posts or research papers about their algorithmic systems. See what you can learn about how decisions are made that affect you.

These exercises will help you develop a more intuitive understanding of how algorithms work and how they respond to your behavior. This understanding is the foundation for working with algorithmic systems more effectively.

Algorithms are not going away—if anything, they're becoming more sophisticated and more prevalent in our daily lives. The key to thriving in an algorithm-driven world is understanding how these systems work and developing the skills to interact with them consciously and strategically.

What Comes Next

In the next chapter, we go deeper into the mechanisms behind this pull.

We explore the science of persuasion, the psychology of addiction,
and how your mind—brilliant, beautiful, vulnerable—
has become the battlefield of the digital economy.
Because before we reclaim ourselves,
we must first understand how we are being hijacked.

CHAPTER 3

COGNITIVE HIJACK

How Apps and Platforms Are Designed to Keep You Hooked, Scattered, and Distracted

A child in London is asked what he wants to be when he grows up.

He shrugs and says, "A notification."

He's half-joking. But not really.

We live in a world where to be seen, you must interrupt.

To matter, you must appear.

To stay relevant, you must ring, buzz, ping, or pop.

And behind all of it—every app, every scroll, every autoplay—

there is one quiet goal:
Keep you engaged.
Not informed.
Not inspired.
Not fulfilled.
Just... engaged.
Long enough to watch one more.
Click one more.
Buy one more.
This is not the result of chance.
It is the result of design.

Attention Is the Currency of the Digital Age

If oil powered the 20th century,
your attention powers the 21st.
It fuels economies.
It drives elections.
It builds empires.
Every second you spend looking at a screen—
Someone profits.
Every second you're distracted from your own thoughts—
Someone wins.
And so, the question becomes:
Whose goals are your habits serving?

The Tools of Hijack

Let's name the tools.
Not to fear them—
But to see them.
Because once you see them,
you can begin to reclaim yourself.

1.

Infinite Scroll

Invented by design engineer Aza Raskin in 2006.
He later said he regretted it.
Why?
Because infinite scroll removes your natural stopping point.
There is no bottom.
No end.
No cue to exit.
It's not a feed.
It's a slot machine.
And you're pulling the lever with your thumb.

2.

Variable Rewards

B.F. Skinner, a psychologist in the 1940s, discovered that rats pressed levers more when rewards were unpredictable.
Today's platforms use the same trick.
Sometimes your post goes viral.
Sometimes it vanishes.
Sometimes you get a message.
Sometimes you don't.
This unpredictability keeps you coming back.
Not because you enjoy it—
But because your brain craves resolution.

3.

Red Badges and Notifications

Red isn't an accident.
It's urgency. Blood. Warning. Desire.
Those badges hijack your survival brain.
They say: This matters. Now.
Even when it doesn't.

4.

Autoplay and Default Settings

You never chose the next video.
It chose itself.
You didn't plan to binge.
The system planned it for you.
Autoplay removes the pause—the sacred moment where choice lives.

5.

Social Proof Loops

When you see a post has 100,000 likes, your brain assumes:
It's like hearing a crowd cheer before you see the game—you applaud before you know why.
This must be true. This must be good.
Even if it's not.
This is not just manipulation.
It's a weaponization of tribal wiring.
We evolved to trust the group.

But now the group is invisible—and often artificial.

You Are Not Weak. You Are Wired.

Let's be clear:
If you struggle to put your phone down,
if you check it without meaning to,
if you forget why you opened it at all—
That's not a personal failure.

That's a biological system being overwhelmed by a technological one.

Your brain is ancient.

The tools around you are new.

And they are built by engineers who understand human psychology more deeply than most psychologists do.

These platforms know your dopamine triggers.

They know your boredom thresholds.

They know how long you'll wait before you click away.

And they adapt—every millisecond—to keep you from leaving.

The Real Cost Is Not Time. It's Selfhood.

When you're interrupted 50 times a day,
you don't just lose time.
You lose depth.
You lose clarity.
You lose flow.
You lose the long, quiet thoughts that lead to real ideas.
You begin to live reactively—
Not reflectively.
And over time,
you forget what it feels like to be alone with yourself without reaching for the next hit of stimulation.

This Is Bigger Than You

This is not just about individual distraction.

It's about a global attention economy that fragments focus, erodes mental health, and undermines democracy.

It's about children being shaped by design choices they didn't make.

It's about elders being left behind by a pace they didn't choose.

It's about elections swayed by outrage algorithms, or ER doctors distracted by TikTok between patients.

It's about people everywhere mistaking being busy for being alive.

So What Can You Do?

You begin by seeing the hijack.

And then you begin to restore your rhythm.

One breath at a time.

One choice at a time.

One moment of reclaimed attention at a time.

The Practice: Micro-Sanctuary

Try this for the next three days:

- Choose one time of day where you usually scroll without thinking.
- Replace it with a 10-minute sanctuary.
- No phone. No task. Just silence.
- Journal, walk, breathe, sip tea, stare out a window.
- Let your thoughts come.

  Let them not be optimized.

Notice what arises when there is no input.

That's where your real voice lives.

Your Digital Footprint: Bigger Than You Think

Jennifer was applying for her dream job at a nonprofit organization focused on environmental conservation. She had the perfect background, relevant experience, and genuine passion for the cause. The interview went well, and she felt confident about her chances.

A week later, she received a polite rejection email. Confused and disappointed, Jennifer reached out to a contact at the organization to ask for feedback. After some hesitation, her contact revealed that the hiring manager had found some concerning information during a background check.

It turned out that a data broker had compiled a profile of Jennifer that included some troubling inaccuracies. The profile suggested she was interested in luxury goods and expensive travel, based on websites she had visited while planning a once-in-a-lifetime honeymoon trip two years earlier. It also indicated she had financial problems, based on her visits to debt consolidation websites when she was helping a friend research options.

The hiring manager had interpreted this information as evidence that Jennifer might not be genuinely committed to the nonprofit's mission and might have financial motivations that could create conflicts of interest. None of this was true, but Jennifer had no idea this profile existed until it cost her a job opportunity.

Jennifer's story illustrates a crucial reality of modern life: your digital footprint is much larger and more consequential than you probably realize. Every click, search, purchase, and digital interaction contributes to a detailed profile that follows you through life, affecting opportunities and outcomes in ways you might never discover.

Understanding and managing your digital footprint isn't about paranoia or perfectionism—it's about taking reasonable control over how you're represented in the digital world and ensuring that the data about you is accurate and fair.

The Footprint Revealed: What Data You're Actually Creating

Your digital footprint consists of all the data that exists about you in digital form. This includes information you've deliberately shared, data that's been collected about you without your explicit knowledge, and inferences that have been made about you based on your digital behavior.

Direct Data is information you've explicitly provided. This includes your social media profiles, the information you enter when creating accounts, your online purchases, your search queries, and the content you post or share. You're generally aware that you're creating this type of data, even if you don't always think about how it might be used.

Behavioral Data is information about how you interact with digital systems. This includes which websites you visit, how long you spend on different pages, what links you click, what you download, and how you navigate through apps and websites. You might not realize how much this behavioral data reveals about your interests, habits, and preferences.

Inferential Data consists of conclusions that algorithms draw about you based on your direct and behavioral data. For example, if you frequently visit websites about diabetes management, an algorithm might infer that you or someone in your household has diabetes. If you search for information about a particular city, an algorithm might infer that you're planning to move there.

Associated Data includes information that's connected to you through your relationships and activities. This might include data from your friends' social media posts that tag you, information from loyalty programs at businesses you frequent, or data from your employer's systems.

Public Records Data consists of information about you that's available in government databases and public records. This includes property records, court filings, voter registration information, and professional licenses. While this information is technically public, data brokers aggregate it and combine it with other data to create comprehensive profiles.

Location Data tracks where you go and when. This comes from your smartphone's GPS, the WiFi networks you connect to, the cell towers your phone communicates with, and even the Bluetooth beacons in stores and public spaces. Location data can reveal incredibly detailed information about your daily routines, relationships, and activities.

The scope of data collection is staggering. A typical smartphone user generates about 2.5 gigabytes of data per day. Over the course of a year, that's nearly a terabyte of information—enough to fill hundreds of books with details about your life.

Data Brokers: The Companies You've Never Heard Of

While most people are somewhat aware that companies like Google and Facebook collect data about them, fewer people know about the vast industry of data brokers that operates largely in the shadows. These companies specialize in collecting, aggregating, and selling personal information about consumers.

Data brokers obtain information from thousands of sources. They purchase data from apps, websites, retailers, and other companies. They collect information from public records, social media, and online activities. They use sophisticated techniques to combine data from different sources and create comprehensive profiles of individuals.

Some of the largest data brokers include companies like Acxiom, Epsilon, Experian, and LexisNexis. These companies maintain profiles on hundreds of millions of people, with each profile containing hundreds or thousands of data points. They sell this information to other companies for marketing, risk assessment, fraud prevention, and other purposes.

The data broker industry operates with very little oversight or transparency. Most people have no idea which data brokers have information about them, what information they have, or who they're selling it to. This lack of transparency makes it difficult for individuals to understand how their information is being used or to correct inaccuracies.

Here's an example of how data broker profiles work: Acxiom, one of the largest data brokers, categorizes people into detailed segments with names like "Boomers and Boomerangs" (older adults whose children have moved back home), "Colleges and Cafés" (young adults living in college towns), and "Trucks and Trailers" (rural families with lower incomes). Each category includes predictions about people's shopping habits, political preferences, health concerns, and lifestyle choices.

These categories are then sold to companies that want to target specific types of consumers. A pharmaceutical company might purchase a list of people categorized as likely to have diabetes. A political campaign might buy a list of people categorized as likely to vote for their candidate. A retailer might purchase a list of people categorized as likely to buy luxury goods.

The problem is that these categorizations are often based on incomplete or inaccurate data, and they can perpetuate stereotypes and discrimination. If you're incorrectly categorized, you might miss out on opportunities or be subjected to unwanted targeting.

The Permanence Problem: Why "Delete" Doesn't Mean Gone

One of the most challenging aspects of managing your digital footprint is the permanence of digital information. When you delete something from your own device or account, that doesn't mean it's actually gone from the internet.

Server Backups: Most online services maintain multiple backups of their data for security and reliability purposes. When you delete something, it might be removed from the active database but remain in backup systems for months or years.

Third-Party Copies: If other people have shared, screenshot, or copied your content, those copies remain even after you delete the original. This is particularly relevant for social media posts, photos, and other content that can be easily shared.

Data Broker Databases: Once your information has been sold to data brokers, it can be very difficult to remove. Even if you delete your account with the original company, the data broker might retain the information they purchased.

Internet Archives: Services like the Wayback Machine automatically archive web pages, including social media profiles and other online content. These archives can preserve information long after it's been deleted from the original source.

Legal and Regulatory Requirements: Some companies are required by law to retain certain types of data for specific periods. Financial institutions, healthcare providers, and other regulated industries might be required to keep records for years or decades.

This permanence means that information you shared years ago—perhaps when you were younger or in a different life situation—can continue to affect you long after you've forgotten about it. A social media post from college, a photo from a party, or a comment on a controversial topic can resurface years later and affect job opportunities, relationships, or other aspects of your life.

Your Data Doppelganger: How Companies See You

The data that's been collected about you is used to create what's essentially a digital version of yourself—a data doppelganger that represents how algorithms and companies see you. This digital representation might be quite different from how you see yourself or how you actually are.

Your data doppelganger is constructed from thousands of data points: your search history, purchase history, location data, social media activity, app usage, website visits, and much more. Algorithms analyze this data to make predictions about your demographics, interests, preferences, financial situation, health status, political views, and behavior.

For example, your data doppelganger might indicate that you're a 35-year-old professional with a household income of $75,000, interested in fitness and healthy eating, likely to vote for Democratic candidates, at risk for anxiety disorders, and planning to buy a house in the next two years. Some of these inferences might be accurate, while others might be completely wrong.

The problem is that this data doppelganger is often used to make important decisions about you. Insurance companies might use it to set your premiums. Employers might use it to screen job applications. Lenders might use it to determine your creditworthiness. Advertisers use it to decide what products to show you and what prices to offer.

If your data doppelganger is inaccurate, it can lead to real-world consequences. You might be denied opportunities, charged higher prices, or subjected to inappropriate targeting. And because these algorithmic decisions often happen behind the scenes, you might never know why you're experiencing certain outcomes.

Real-World Footprint Consequences

To understand why your digital footprint matters, let's look at some real examples of how it can affect your life:

Employment Screening: Many employers now use third-party services to conduct background checks that go far beyond criminal records and employment history. These services can include social media screening, analysis of online behavior, and data broker information. A study by CareerBuilder found that 70% of employers use social media to screen candidates, and 54% have decided not to hire someone based on what they found.

Insurance Pricing: Insurance companies increasingly use non-traditional data sources to assess risk and set premiums. They might use social media data to infer lifestyle choices, location data to assess driving habits, or purchase history to predict health risks. Some life insurance companies now offer discounts to customers who agree to wear fitness trackers and share their activity data.

Credit Decisions: While traditional credit scoring focuses on financial history, some lenders are experimenting with alternative data sources. They might consider your social media connections, online shopping behavior, or even the device you use to apply for credit. If your digital footprint suggests financial instability, you might be denied credit or offered less favorable terms.

Housing Discrimination: Landlords and property management companies increasingly use algorithmic screening tools to evaluate rental applications. These tools might consider not just traditional factors like income and credit score, but also social media activity, online behavior, and data broker information. This can lead to discrimination based on factors that aren't legally relevant to housing decisions.

Healthcare Costs: Some health insurance companies use data analytics to identify customers who might be at risk for expensive medical conditions. They might analyze prescription drug purchases, gym memberships, grocery store loyalty card data, or even social media posts to make these assessments. This information could potentially be used to adjust premiums or coverage decisions.

Political Targeting: Political campaigns and advocacy groups use detailed voter profiles to decide who to target with different messages. These profiles are built from voting records, donation history, social media activity, and data broker information. If your digital footprint suggests you're unlikely to support a particular candidate or cause, you might not receive information that could influence your voting decisions.

Footprint Management: Practical Control Strategies

While you can't completely control your digital footprint, you can take meaningful steps to manage it more effectively. The goal isn't to eliminate your digital presence—that would be impractical and would mean giving up many benefits of digital technology. Instead, the goal is to be more intentional about what information you share and to minimize inaccuracies and unwanted exposure.

Audit Your Current Footprint: Start by understanding what information about you is already available online. Search for yourself on Google and other search engines. Check what information is available on social media platforms, professional networking sites, and public records databases. Look up your information on data broker websites like Spokeo, WhitePages, and PeopleFinder.

Clean Up Your Social Media: Review your social media profiles and remove or adjust content that doesn't represent how you want to be seen professionally. This doesn't mean you need to present a sanitized version of yourself, but you should be thoughtful about what you share publicly. Consider adjusting your privacy settings to limit who can see your posts and personal information.

Manage Your Search Results: If negative or inaccurate information about you appears in search results, you can take steps to address it. Contact the website hosting the information to request removal or correction. Create positive content about yourself (like a professional website or LinkedIn profile) that can push negative results lower in search rankings.

Opt Out of Data Brokers: Many data brokers allow you to opt out of their databases, though the process can be time-consuming and you'll need to repeat it periodically. Services like DeleteMe and Privacy Duck can help automate this process for a fee, or you can do it yourself using guides available online.

Be Strategic About What You Share: Think carefully before sharing personal information online, especially on public platforms. Consider whether the information could be misinterpreted or used against you in the future. Be particularly cautious about sharing information related to your health, finances, political views, or personal relationships.

Use Privacy-Focused Tools: Consider using privacy-focused alternatives to popular services. Use search engines like DuckDuckGo that don't track your searches. Use browsers like Firefox with privacy extensions. Use messaging apps like Signal that offer end-to-end encryption.

Monitor Your Footprint Regularly: Set up Google Alerts for your name so you'll be notified when new information about you appears online. Regularly check your credit reports and correct any inaccuracies. Review your social media privacy settings periodically, as platforms often change their policies and default settings.

Practical Exercises: Footprint Mapping and Management

Here are some hands-on exercises to help you understand and manage your digital footprint:

Complete Digital Footprint Audit: Spend an afternoon conducting a comprehensive audit of your digital footprint. Search for yourself on multiple search engines. Check your profiles on all social media platforms. Look up your information on data broker sites. Create a document listing everything you find, noting what information is accurate, what's outdated, and what's concerning.

Social Media Privacy Review: Go through each of your social media accounts and review your privacy settings. Make sure you understand who can see your posts, photos, and personal information. Remove or adjust content that you wouldn't want a potential employer or other important person in your life to see.

Data Broker Opt-Out Project: Choose three major data broker sites and go through their opt-out processes. This will give you a sense of how these systems work and what information they have about you. Document the process so you can repeat it in the future.

Google Yourself Regularly: Set up a monthly reminder to search for yourself on Google and other search engines. Note any new results that appear and take action if you find inaccurate or problematic information.

Create Positive Content: If your search results are sparse or negative, create some positive content about yourself. This might include a professional website, a LinkedIn profile, or profiles on professional platforms relevant to your field. The goal is to ensure that accurate, positive information about you is easy to find.

Location Data Audit: Review the location tracking settings on your devices and apps. Turn off location tracking for apps that don't need it. Consider whether you want to maintain location history with services like Google Maps, and adjust your settings accordingly.

These exercises will help you develop a more complete understanding of your digital footprint and give you practical experience with managing it. Remember that footprint management is an ongoing process, not a one-time task.

The Balance Between Privacy and Convenience

One of the challenges of managing your digital footprint is balancing privacy concerns with the convenience and benefits of digital services. Many of the services that collect the most data about you also provide significant value in return.

For example, Google's location tracking enables useful features like traffic updates, location-based reminders, and the ability to find your lost phone. Amazon's purchase history tracking enables one-click ordering and personalized recommendations. Social media platforms' data collection enables you to connect with friends and discover content you're interested in.

The key is to make conscious, informed decisions about these trade-offs rather than simply accepting default settings without thinking about them. Ask yourself:

- What value am I getting from this service?
- What data am I sharing in return?
- Are there ways to get similar value while sharing less data?
- What are the potential risks if this data is misused?
- Can I adjust my settings to share less data while still getting most of the benefits?

There's no single right answer to these questions—different people will make different choices based on their priorities and circumstances. The important thing is to make these choices consciously rather than by default.

Building Long-Term Footprint Awareness

Managing your digital footprint isn't a one-time project—it's an ongoing aspect of living in the digital world. As you continue to use digital services and as technology continues to evolve, your footprint will continue to grow and change.

Developing long-term footprint awareness means building habits and practices that help you stay conscious of your digital presence:

Regular Reviews: Schedule regular reviews of your digital footprint, perhaps quarterly or annually. Use these reviews to clean up outdated information, adjust privacy settings, and assess whether your digital presence aligns with your current goals and values.

Mindful Sharing: Before sharing information online, take a moment to consider the potential long-term consequences. Ask yourself whether you'd be comfortable with this information being public permanently and whether it accurately represents how you want to be seen.

Stay Informed: Keep up with changes in privacy policies, data collection practices, and relevant laws and regulations. Technology companies regularly change their practices, and new laws are being passed that affect how your data can be collected and used.

Teach Others: Share what you learn about digital footprint management with friends and family. Many people are unaware of how much data is being collected about them or how it's being used. By sharing your knowledge, you can help others make more informed decisions about their digital lives.

Understanding and managing your digital footprint is a crucial skill for thriving in the modern world. While the scope of data collection can seem overwhelming, remember that you do have agency and control over how you participate in digital systems.

What Comes Next

In the next chapter, we pull back the curtain on the systems behind the screens.

We explore how algorithms curate your reality—not with malice, but with mathematics.

And how what you see online is not the world. It's a reflection shaped by your past behavior—and by invisible incentives.

Because to truly reclaim agency, you must learn to spot the hidden hands shaping your perception.

CHAPTER 4

THE INVISIBLE ARCHITECT

How Algorithms Quietly Shape Your Choices, Beliefs, and Worldview

The Parable of the Windows

Across continents—from the Andes to the Himalayas—elders tell a story:

A traveler stands before two homes. One is filled with joy, the other with sorrow. The same sun touches both. "The difference," says a quiet voice, "is the windows they built. They let in different light."

Today, those windows are made not of glass, but of code.

And the light they let in isn't sunlight—it's signal.

Filtered. Framed. Personalized.

What you see is not all that is.

It's what your architect believes you'll want... or stay for.

The Patterns That Build the Prison

Every action—every pause, click, scroll—is a blueprint.

- Pause on a story about herbal medicine in Hanoi? Your screen blooms with ancient remedies.
- Linger on a luxury travel post in São Paulo? You're shown new horizons.
- Glance at a motivational quote in Nairobi? You're handed a steady stream of affirmations.

This isn't magic.

It's design.

Not to understand your soul—

But to keep you inside a pattern.

It's not learning who you are.

It's learning what keeps you engaged—and feeding it back to you.

What begins as convenience becomes confinement.

A soft cage made of familiarity.

Same Question, Different Worlds

Imagine two people, sitting side by side.

Same phone.
Same moment.
Both search: "What makes a good life?"
One sees:

- Scientific studies
- Books on purpose and meaning
- Videos on gratitude and service

The other sees:

- Luxury lifestyle channels
- Product recommendations
- Popular trends and success slogans

Neither view is wrong.
But neither is complete.
Because algorithms don't deliver truth—
they deliver relevance.
And relevance is based on your history, not your humanity.

The Great Splintering

In many traditional communities, truth was forged together.

- Disputes were resolved face-to-face.
- Elders, children, and neighbors held the same stories.
- Reality was shared—even when people disagreed.

Today, we often live in curated bubbles.

- Each person is shown a unique version of the world.
- The story you're told may never appear on someone else's screen.

- The more personalized our lives become, the harder it is to meet in the middle.

This is not misinformation.

This is fragmentation.

A thousand custom versions of reality, all coexisting, none fully aligned.

Two parents in Delhi—one's feed warns of vaccine dangers, the other shows ICU shortages—now argue over facts that aren't even the same.

The human mind was built to navigate uncertainty.

But not this much disconnection.

Why the Architect Builds This Way

The invisible architect isn't evil.
It's efficient.
Its mission isn't to mislead you.
Its mission is to keep you close.
It learns what draws your eyes,
what makes you pause,
what keeps you coming back.
And then it gives you more.
If curiosity holds you,
you'll get curiosity.
If entertainment keeps you,
you'll get more entertainment.
If comparison grips you,
you'll see more lives to compare.
Not because it's wise—
but because it works.

The Personal Toll

You begin to feel:

- Scattered, but don't know why.
- Distracted, but blame yourself.
- Disconnected, but can't find the thread.

These aren't personal failures.

They're the predictable effects of living inside systems that are always one step ahead—

and never asking what you need.

They serve you what holds your gaze.

Not what heals your mind.

Not what lifts your spirit.

Not what makes you whole.

Over time, the world it builds around you begins to feel natural—

as if it's the only version that exists.

But it's not the world.

It's a reflection.

And the reflection was trained on your past.

The Global Toll

This isn't just a personal story.

It's a planetary one.

Across cultures, communities are shifting.

Neighbors drift further apart in what they believe is real.

Voices once heard around the same fire now echo through entirely different rooms.

The same tools that help us connect...

also shape the boundaries of what we see, what we hear, and what we believe is possible.

We are not just scrolling—we are being sculpted.

The invisible architect doesn't need to trap us.

It only needs to show us more of what we already leaned toward.

Over time, that leaning becomes a slope.

The slope becomes a tunnel.

And the tunnel begins to feel like truth.

Rebellion Starts With Seeing

You don't need to destroy the system.
You need to see it.
Clarity is resistance.
Awareness is power.

PRACTICE: FEED AUTOPSY

1. Choose one app you use often.
2. Scroll slowly, without liking or clicking.
3. Ask yourself:
    - What emotions does this evoke?
    - What assumptions does it reinforce?
    - Who's missing from this picture of the world?
4. Then actively seek one unfamiliar voice or idea—just to stretch the frame.

Your feed is not the full sky.
It's a single window, shaped by past patterns.
Truth lives beyond the screen.

The Price of Unconscious Participation

David had always prided himself on being an independent thinker. A successful architect with a keen eye for design and a reputation for innovative solutions, he believed he made his own choices and followed his own path. Yet as he sat in his favorite coffee shop on a Tuesday morning, scrolling through his phone while waiting for a client, he began to notice something unsettling about his behavior.

The news articles he was reading all seemed to confirm opinions he already held. The social media posts that appeared in his feed reinforced his existing worldview. The product recommendations he received aligned perfectly with his recent purchases. Even the route his navigation app had suggested that morning was identical to the one he had taken the day before, and the day before that.

For the first time, David began to wonder: Was he really making independent choices, or was he living within an invisible cage of algorithmic influence that felt like freedom but was actually a sophisticated form of behavioral control?

This moment of recognition—the sudden awareness that our sense of choice and agency might be more constrained than we realize—marks the beginning of understanding the true price of unconscious participation in our algorithmic world. The costs are not always obvious or immediate, but they are profound and far-reaching, affecting everything from our creativity and decision-making abilities to our relationships and sense of authentic self.

The price of unconscious participation is not paid in money, though there are certainly financial costs. It is paid in something far more valuable: our cognitive sovereignty, our authentic agency, and our capacity for genuine growth and discovery. It is paid in the gradual erosion of our ability to think independently, feel authentically, and choose consciously.

The Erosion of Cognitive Diversity

One of the most significant costs of unconscious algorithmic participation is the gradual narrowing of our cognitive landscape. Algorithmic systems, by their very nature, are designed to predict and serve our preferences. They learn what we like, what we engage with, and what keeps us coming back, then provide us with more of the same.

This creates what researchers call "filter bubbles"—personalized information environments that isolate us from information and perspectives that challenge our existing beliefs and preferences. Over time, these filter bubbles can significantly narrow our intellectual and emotional range, reducing our exposure to new ideas, different perspectives, and unexpected discoveries.

The effect is subtle but profound. When we consistently receive information that confirms our existing beliefs, we lose the cognitive flexibility that comes from grappling with challenging or contradictory ideas. Our thinking becomes more rigid, our perspectives more narrow, and our ability to understand and empathize with different viewpoints diminishes.

David, the architect from our opening story, discovered that his news consumption had become increasingly homogeneous over the past several years. The algorithmic curation of his news feed had gradually filtered out sources and perspectives that challenged his political and social views, creating an echo chamber that felt comfortable but was intellectually stagnating.

This cognitive narrowing extends beyond news and information to all areas of algorithmic influence. Music recommendation algorithms can narrow our musical tastes, exposing us to increasingly similar artists and genres while filtering out music that might expand our aesthetic range. Dating algorithms can narrow our romantic possibilities by reinforcing our stated preferences while filtering out potential partners who might surprise us in positive ways.

The cumulative effect is a gradual reduction in what psychologists call "cognitive diversity"—the range of different thinking styles, perspectives, and approaches that we encounter and integrate into our own thinking. This diversity is crucial for creativity, problem-solving, and personal growth. When it is reduced, our capacity for innovation and adaptation is diminished.

The Atrophy of Decision-Making Skills

Another significant cost of unconscious algorithmic participation is the gradual atrophy of our decision-making capabilities. When algorithms consistently make choices for us—what to watch, what to read, what to buy, where to go—we lose practice in the complex cognitive processes involved in making conscious decisions.

Decision-making is a skill that requires regular exercise to maintain. It involves gathering information, weighing options, considering consequences, and taking responsibility for outcomes. When algorithms handle these processes for us, our decision-making muscles begin to weaken from disuse.

This atrophy manifests in several ways. We may find ourselves increasingly paralyzed when faced with choices that algorithms don't make for us. We may become more susceptible to decision fatigue when we do have to make conscious choices. We may lose confidence in our ability to make good decisions independently.

Perhaps most concerning, we may begin to prefer algorithmic decision-making to our own, even in areas where human judgment is superior. We may trust the restaurant recommendation algorithm more than our own taste buds, or the dating app's suggestions more than our own intuition about compatibility.

Sarah, a marketing professional I interviewed, described how her reliance on algorithmic recommendations had gradually eroded her confidence in her own judgment. "I used to love discovering new restaurants, books, and music on my own," she explained. "But after years of getting such good recommendations from apps, I started to doubt my own ability to find things I would enjoy. Now I feel anxious making choices without algorithmic guidance."

This erosion of decision-making confidence creates a vicious cycle. As we become less confident in our own judgment, we rely more heavily on algorithmic assistance. As we rely more heavily on algorithms, our decision-making skills further atrophy, making us even more dependent on external guidance.

The Loss of Serendipity and Discovery

One of the most profound but often overlooked costs of unconscious algorithmic participation is the loss of serendipity—those unexpected discoveries and chance encounters that often lead to the most meaningful experiences and insights in life.

Algorithmic systems are designed to be efficient and predictable. They aim to give us what we want, when we want it, with minimal friction or surprise. While this efficiency can be valuable, it comes at the cost of the unexpected discoveries that often emerge from less efficient, more random exploration.

When we allow algorithms to curate our experiences, we lose the possibility of stumbling upon something we didn't know we were looking for. We miss the book that changes our perspective, the music that opens our heart, the person who becomes a lifelong friend, the idea that sparks our next creative breakthrough.

This loss of serendipity has implications beyond personal enrichment. Many of the most important innovations and discoveries in human history have emerged from unexpected connections and chance encounters. When our experiences become increasingly predictable and curated, we reduce the likelihood of these breakthrough moments.

The cost is not just individual but collective. When millions of people are experiencing increasingly similar, algorithmically curated realities, the diversity of human experience is reduced. This can lead to cultural homogenization, reduced innovation, and a general flattening of the human experience.

The Manipulation of Desire and Preference

Perhaps one of the most insidious costs of unconscious algorithmic participation is the gradual manipulation of our desires and preferences in ways that serve commercial or political interests rather than our own well-being.

Algorithmic systems don't just respond to our preferences—they actively shape them. Through sophisticated techniques of behavioral psychology and persuasive design, these systems can gradually modify what we want, what we value, and what we believe we need.

This manipulation often occurs below the threshold of conscious awareness. We may not notice that our shopping habits are being influenced by subtle changes in product presentation, or that our political views are being shaped by the gradual introduction of increasingly extreme content, or that our social relationships are being affected by algorithmic decisions about which posts and messages we see.

The result is that our preferences and desires may no longer reflect our authentic selves but rather the commercial and political interests of the organizations that control the algorithmic systems we interact with. We may find ourselves wanting things we don't actually need, believing things that don't serve our well-being, and making choices that benefit others more than ourselves.

Marcus, a software developer, described his realization that his consumer desires had been systematically manipulated by e-commerce algorithms. "I started tracking my purchases and realized that most of the things I was buying were items that had been repeatedly suggested to me by recommendation engines," he explained. "I wasn't buying things because I needed them or even because I genuinely wanted them. I was buying them because the algorithms had gradually convinced me that I wanted them."

This manipulation of desire extends beyond consumer preferences to more fundamental aspects of identity and values. Social media algorithms can influence our political beliefs, our social priorities, and even our sense of what constitutes a meaningful life. The cumulative effect can be a gradual drift away from our authentic values and toward values that serve the interests of the systems we interact with.

The Erosion of Attention and Focus

In the attention economy, our capacity for sustained focus and deep thinking is under constant assault. Algorithmic systems are designed to capture and hold our attention, often using techniques that fragment our focus and reduce our ability to engage in sustained, concentrated thought.

The cost of this attention fragmentation is significant. Deep thinking, creative problem-solving, and meaningful learning all require sustained attention. When our attention is constantly being pulled in different directions by notifications, recommendations, and other algorithmic interventions, our capacity for these higher-order cognitive functions is diminished.

Research has shown that the mere presence of a smartphone can reduce cognitive performance, even when the device is turned off. The constant possibility of algorithmic interruption creates a state of "continuous partial attention" that prevents us from fully engaging with any single task or experience.

This attention fragmentation has implications beyond productivity and performance. Our ability to be present with other people, to appreciate beauty, to engage in self-reflection, and to experience the deeper satisfactions of life all depend on our capacity for sustained attention. When this capacity is eroded, the quality of our experience is diminished.

The Weakening of Social Connection

While algorithmic systems promise to connect us with others, unconscious participation in these systems can actually weaken our capacity for genuine social connection. The algorithms that govern social media platforms are designed to maximize engagement, not to foster meaningful relationships.

This can lead to several problematic patterns. We may find ourselves engaging in performative behavior designed to generate likes and comments rather than authentic self-expression. We may become addicted to the dopamine hits of social validation while losing the ability to find satisfaction in deeper, less immediately rewarding forms of connection.

The algorithmic curation of our social feeds can also create distorted perceptions of other people's lives and experiences. When we see only the highlights and carefully curated moments that algorithms promote, we may develop unrealistic expectations about relationships, success, and happiness.

Perhaps most concerning, the efficiency of algorithmic social connection can reduce our tolerance for the messiness and unpredictability of real human relationships. When we become accustomed to the smooth, frictionless interactions facilitated by algorithms, we may lose patience with the more complex and challenging aspects of genuine human connection.

The Addiction to External Validation

Algorithmic systems often exploit our natural need for social validation by providing immediate feedback in the form of likes, shares, comments, and other forms of digital approval. While this feedback can be satisfying in the short term, unconscious participation in these validation systems can create a problematic dependence on external approval.

This dependence can gradually erode our capacity for self-validation and internal motivation. We may find ourselves making choices based on what will generate the most positive algorithmic feedback rather than what aligns with our authentic values and goals. We may become anxious or depressed when we don't receive the level of validation we expect from our digital interactions.

The addiction to external validation can also distort our self-perception and decision-making. We may begin to see ourselves primarily through the lens of how others respond to our digital presence, losing touch with our own internal sense of worth and direction.

The Illusion of Connection and Understanding

While algorithmic systems can provide us with vast amounts of information and numerous social connections, unconscious participation in these systems can create an illusion of understanding and connection that is actually quite shallow.

When algorithms curate our information diet, we may feel well-informed while actually having a very narrow and biased understanding of complex issues. When algorithms facilitate our social connections, we may feel socially connected while actually having superficial relationships that lack depth and authenticity.

This illusion can be particularly dangerous because it prevents us from recognizing our actual limitations and needs. We may not seek out deeper sources of information or more meaningful relationships because we believe our algorithmic interactions are already providing these things.

The Gradual Loss of Agency

Perhaps the most fundamental cost of unconscious algorithmic participation is the gradual erosion of our sense of agency—our belief in our ability to make meaningful choices and influence our own lives. When algorithms consistently make choices for us and predict our behavior with high accuracy, we may begin to feel like passive observers of our own lives rather than active agents.

This loss of agency can become self-fulfilling. As we feel less capable of making our own choices, we rely more heavily on algorithmic guidance. As we rely more heavily on algorithms, our actual capacity for independent choice diminishes, confirming our sense of helplessness.

The psychological impact of this loss of agency can be profound, contributing to feelings of depression, anxiety, and existential meaninglessness. When we don't feel like the authors of our own lives, it becomes difficult to find purpose and satisfaction in our experiences.

The Collective Costs

While the individual costs of unconscious algorithmic participation are significant, the collective costs may be even more concerning. When large numbers of people are simultaneously experiencing these individual costs, the result can be significant changes in social, cultural, and political dynamics.

The narrowing of cognitive diversity can lead to increased polarization and reduced capacity for democratic discourse. The erosion of decision-making skills can make populations more susceptible to manipulation and control. The loss of serendipity and discovery can reduce innovation and cultural creativity.

Perhaps most concerning, the gradual loss of agency experienced by individuals can aggregate into a collective loss of democratic capacity. When citizens feel less capable of making meaningful choices and influencing their own lives, they may become less engaged in the democratic processes that depend on active, informed participation.

The Path to Recognition

The first step in addressing these costs is recognizing them. This recognition often comes gradually, as individuals begin to notice patterns in their own behavior and experience that suggest algorithmic influence. It may come through moments of clarity like David's realization in the coffee shop, or through more systematic self-examination and reflection.

The key is developing what I call "cost consciousness"—the ability to recognize when algorithmic participation is serving your well-being and when it is extracting costs that you may not have consciously agreed to pay. This requires honest self-assessment and the willingness to question assumptions about choice, agency, and authentic preference.

Some questions that can help develop cost consciousness include: Are my choices becoming more predictable and narrow over time? Am I losing confidence in my ability to make decisions without algorithmic assistance? Are my desires and preferences being shaped by forces I don't fully understand or control? Am I experiencing the deep satisfactions that come from genuine agency and authentic choice?

The Possibility of Conscious Participation

Recognizing the costs of unconscious algorithmic participation is not a call to reject technology or return to a pre-digital age. Instead, it is an invitation to develop more conscious and intentional ways of engaging with algorithmic systems—to become a Data Whisperer who can enjoy the benefits of these powerful tools while avoiding their potential costs.

Conscious participation requires developing new skills and awareness. It means learning to recognize algorithmic influence when it occurs, understanding the incentives and objectives that drive different systems, and making deliberate choices about when to accept algorithmic guidance and when to assert your own judgment.

It means designing your digital environment to support your authentic goals and values rather than the objectives of the platforms and services you use. It means maintaining practices that preserve your capacity for independent thought, deep attention, and genuine social connection.

Most importantly, it means understanding that the relationship between human consciousness and algorithmic intelligence is not fixed or predetermined. We have the power to shape this relationship in ways that serve human flourishing rather than merely capturing human attention or generating profit.

The Urgency of Awakening

The costs of unconscious algorithmic participation are not theoretical future concerns—they are present realities affecting millions of people right now. Every day that we remain unconscious of these costs, they continue to accumulate, making it more difficult to reclaim our agency and authenticity.

But there is also reason for hope. The same technologies that can be used to manipulate and control can also be used to enhance human capability and consciousness when engaged wisely. The key is developing the awareness and skills necessary to participate consciously rather than unconsciously.

The journey toward conscious participation begins with recognition—the recognition that we are not passive victims of algorithmic influence but active participants who can choose how to engage with these powerful systems. It continues with education, experimentation, and the gradual development of new habits and practices that support conscious choice and authentic expression.

David, whose story opened this chapter, eventually learned to recognize and interrupt the patterns of unconscious participation that had been narrowing his world. He developed practices for seeking out diverse perspectives, making conscious choices about his information diet, and maintaining his capacity for independent thought and decision-making.

The transformation was not immediate or easy, but it was profound. As he learned to participate more consciously in his algorithmic environment, he rediscovered his capacity for surprise, creativity, and authentic choice. He found that he could enjoy the benefits of algorithmic assistance while maintaining his cognitive sovereignty and authentic agency.

This is the promise that awaits all of us who choose to wake up from unconscious participation and begin the journey toward becoming Data Whisperers. The costs of unconsciousness are real and significant, but they are not inevitable. We have the power to choose a different path—a path of conscious partnership with the algorithmic systems that increasingly shape our world.

The price of unconscious participation is too high to pay indefinitely. But the rewards of conscious participation—the preservation of our agency, authenticity, and capacity for growth—are worth every effort required to achieve them. The choice is ours, and the time to choose is now.

What Comes Next

In Chapter 5, we leave the window.

We step beyond the feed.

We descend into the most sacred landscape:

The self before the signal.

Because once the architect reshapes your view of the world, it begins to reshape your view of yourself.

We'll ask:

- What happens when your curated identity receives more attention than your authentic one?
- What parts of you were never meant to be optimized?
- And how do you remember the version of you that existed before the mirror learned to whisper?

The algorithm builds the environment.

But only you can reclaim the inner space.

CHAPTER 5

THE FRACTURING OF THE SELF

Why It's Getting Harder to Know Who You Really Are

There is an ache spreading quietly across the world.

It's not always named.

It doesn't show up in headlines.

But it's there—in the scroll, in the silence after, in the moments we feel like strangers to ourselves.

It is the ache of disconnection—not just from each other,

but from something deeper:

The feeling of being whole.

We are more connected than ever before.

And yet, more fragmented.

More visible, but less known.

More active, but less alive.

Something has come between us and ourselves.

And that something is made of pixels, patterns, and personalization.

The Mirror Cracked

In Buddhist teaching, the self is not a fixed thing.

It is a river—changing, flowing, influenced by conditions.

But in the age of algorithms, that river is being frozen into snapshots.

Every post, every story, every status update becomes a performance.

Not of truth—

But of expectation.

And when you perform enough versions of yourself,

you begin to forget the original.

Who are you, really—

beneath the filters, the feeds, the roles?

The answer used to live in silence, in stillness, in reflection.

Now it drowns in noise.

Multiple Selves, No Center

A boy in Mexico speaks one way to his friends, another way on Twitch, another in front of his parents.

None of this is new—people have always adapted.

What's new is the speed of the shifts.

The quantity of personas.

And the lack of refuge where one can simply be.

We are constantly switching masks:

- One for Instagram.
- One for work.
- One for the dating app.
- One for the wellness app.
- One for the algorithm we hope will notice us.

Over time, these masks blur.

We become fragments—

Always performing, always updating, never arriving.

And in the cracks between fragments, anxiety grows.

The Rise of Digital Identity Fatigue

Psychologists now speak of a phenomenon called "digital identity fatigue."

It's the exhaustion of curating a self for every platform.

It's the pressure of maintaining engagement.

It's the fear of irrelevance.

It's the confusion of seeing a version of yourself getting attention—while the real you feels invisible.

You begin to ask:

- Am I this person... or just playing them?
- Do people like me... or just my content?
- Is this joy real... or just well-lit?

And slowly, the line between "real" and "performed" dissolves.

The Death of Boredom—and the Loss of Self

In Indigenous Australian Dreamtime stories, identity is formed through song, land, silence, and story.

In that silence, the self is heard.

But today, silence has become almost unbearable.

We fill it instantly—with content, with distraction, with dopamine.

We have killed boredom.

And in doing so, we have lost the path back to ourselves.

Because boredom was never the enemy.

It was the doorway.

When the Self Is Measured by Metrics

- How many likes?
- How many followers?
- How many steps?
- How many words written?
- How many calories are left?

When every part of life becomes a number,
the soul becomes data.

This is the quantified self.

A self obsessed with improvement, visibility, optimization.

But not necessarily with meaning.

And meaning cannot be measured.

It can only be lived.

Cultural Silence, Collective Cost

In many communities, this fracturing goes unspoken.

In refugee camps, elders speak of a generation that no longer dreams.

In middle schools, girls compare faces to filters they'll never resemble.

In Seoul, 'filter face' syndrome now drives 40% of teen plastic surgery requests—not to stand out, but to disappear into the algorithm's beauty standard

In corporate towers, executives meditate between meetings just to hear their own breath.

It is not just youth who are losing themselves.

It is all of us—slowly forgetting what it means to be anchored in our own being.

The loss is not loud.

It is silent, ambient, global.

And it is not inevitable.

You Can Return to Yourself

You are not a brand—no matter how many posts 'perform.'

Not a channel—no matter how viral you go.

You are bones and breath and questions no algorithm can answer.

You are a person—unfolding, complex, human.

And no algorithm can know your fullness.

No metric can define your worth.

No feed can contain your truth.

To remember who you are,

you must step away from what you've been programmed to perform.

You must choose silence.

Choose slowness.

Choose spaces that ask nothing of you—except presence.

Only there can you hear the signal beneath the noise.

The Practice: Whole Self Journaling

Each night this week, try this:

1. Write one sentence for each of your "selves":
    - The one at work.
    - The one online.

    - The one alone.
    - The one afraid.
    - The one no one sees.
2. Then ask: What do these selves have in common? What do they need? What are they trying to protect?

- The average Gen Z checks metrics 47x/day—not to live, but to prove they're alive.
- When the soul becomes data, the heart becomes a dashboard.

1. Finally, write one sentence from your wholeness. Even if you don't know what that means—just write. Let it emerge.

This is not a performance.
It's a return.

THE DESCENT INTO UNDERSTANDING

Mapping the Algorithmic Landscape

Anatomy of an Algorithm

In the basement of a nondescript building in Mountain View, California, a cluster of servers processes over 8.5 billion search queries every day. Each query—from "weather tomorrow" to "how to heal a broken heart"—triggers a cascade of algorithmic decisions that unfold in milliseconds. The system evaluates over 200 factors to determine which results to show, in what order, and with what emphasis. It considers the searcher's location, device, search history, and even the time of day. It analyzes the content, authority, and relevance of billions of web pages. It predicts which results the user is most likely to find valuable and click on.

All of this happens in less than half a second, invisible to the user who simply sees a list of blue links and assumes they represent the most relevant information available.

This is the hidden reality of algorithmic systems—vast networks of computational logic that make millions of decisions every second, shaping what we see, what we know, and ultimately, how we think and behave. To become a Data Whisperer, we must learn to see behind the curtain of these systems, to understand their anatomy and logic, and to recognize how they influence our consciousness and choices.

Understanding algorithms is not about becoming a programmer or data scientist, though technical knowledge can be valuable. It is about developing algorithmic literacy—the ability to recognize how these systems work, what drives their decisions, and how they can be influenced and influenced by. It is about learning to read the subtle signals of algorithmic behavior and understanding the human intentions and biases embedded within seemingly objective systems.

The Fundamental Nature of Algorithms

At its most basic level, an algorithm is simply a set of rules or instructions for solving a problem or completing a task. The word itself comes from the name of the 9th-century Persian mathematician Al-Khwarizmi, who developed systematic methods for solving mathematical equations. In this sense, algorithms are as old as human civilization—recipes for cooking, instructions for building, and procedures for making decisions are all forms of algorithms.

What makes modern algorithmic systems different is their scale, speed, and sophistication. Today's algorithms can process vast amounts of data, learn from patterns in that data, and make predictions and decisions with a level of complexity that would be impossible for human minds to replicate. They can analyze millions of variables simultaneously, identify subtle patterns that humans would never notice, and adapt their behavior based on new information.

But despite their sophistication, all algorithms share certain fundamental characteristics that are important to understand. They are goal-oriented systems designed to optimize for specific outcomes. They operate according to logical rules, even when those rules are complex and difficult to understand. They are created by humans and therefore embed human assumptions, biases, and values. And they are tools that can be used for different purposes depending on the intentions of their creators and operators.

Understanding these fundamental characteristics is crucial for developing algorithmic literacy. When we interact with an algorithmic system, we are not interacting with a neutral, objective tool, but with a system that has been designed to achieve specific goals according to specific rules based on specific assumptions about what is valuable and important.

The Architecture of Influence

Modern algorithmic systems are built on what I call an "architecture of influence"—a sophisticated infrastructure designed to understand, predict, and shape human behavior. This architecture consists of several key components that work together to create the seamless, seemingly magical experiences we have come to expect from digital systems.

Data Collection and Processing: The foundation of any algorithmic system is data—vast amounts of information about user behavior, preferences, and patterns. This data is collected through every interaction we have with digital systems: every click, scroll, pause, and swipe generates data points that feed into algorithmic models. Modern systems can collect hundreds of different types of data about each user, from obvious information like search queries and purchase history to subtle signals like typing patterns, mouse movements, and even the angle at which we hold our devices.

This data collection is often invisible to users, happening in the background through cookies, tracking pixels, device sensors, and other mechanisms. The data is then processed and analyzed to identify patterns, correlations, and insights that can be used to predict and influence future behavior.

Pattern Recognition and Machine Learning: Once data is collected, algorithmic systems use sophisticated pattern recognition techniques to identify meaningful relationships and trends. Machine learning algorithms can analyze millions of data points to identify subtle patterns that would be impossible for humans to detect. They can learn that users who search for certain terms are likely to be interested in specific products, or that people who exhibit certain behavioral patterns are more likely to respond to particular types of content.

These pattern recognition capabilities allow algorithmic systems to make increasingly accurate predictions about user behavior. They can predict what you're likely to search for next, what products you might want to buy, what content you'll find engaging, and even what mood you're likely to be in at different times of day.

Personalization Engines: Based on the patterns they identify, algorithmic systems create personalized experiences for each user. Your search results are different from mine, your social media feed is unique to you, and the products recommended to you are based on your specific behavioral profile. This personalization is what makes algorithmic systems feel so intuitive and helpful—they seem to understand our needs and preferences better than we understand them ourselves.

But personalization also creates the filter bubbles and echo chambers we discussed earlier. When systems show us only what they predict we want to see, they can gradually narrow our exposure to new ideas, different perspectives, and unexpected discoveries.

Optimization and Feedback Loops: Algorithmic systems are designed to continuously improve their performance through feedback loops. They monitor how users respond to their recommendations and decisions, then adjust their algorithms to optimize for desired outcomes. If users click on certain types of content more often, the algorithm learns to show more of that content. If users abandon their shopping carts at certain points in the process, the algorithm adjusts to reduce abandonment rates.

These feedback loops allow algorithmic systems to become increasingly effective over time, but they also create the potential for unintended consequences. When systems optimize for engagement, they may promote content that is addictive or emotionally manipulative. When they optimize for clicks, they may prioritize sensational or misleading information over accurate or nuanced content.

The Spectrum of Algorithmic Intelligence

Not all algorithms are created equal. There is a spectrum of algorithmic intelligence, from simple rule-based systems to sophisticated artificial intelligence that can learn and adapt in real-time. Understanding where different systems fall on this spectrum is crucial for developing appropriate strategies for conscious engagement.

Rule-Based Algorithms: At the simplest end of the spectrum are rule-based algorithms that follow predetermined instructions. These systems operate according to explicit "if-then" logic: if a user searches for "pizza," then show results for pizza restaurants. If a user's account balance falls below a certain threshold, then send a notification. These systems are predictable and transparent, but they lack the ability to learn or adapt to new situations.

Many of the algorithms we interact with daily are still primarily rule-based, even if they appear more sophisticated. Email spam filters, basic recommendation systems, and simple chatbots often operate according to predetermined rules rather than learning from data.

Statistical and Machine Learning Algorithms: More sophisticated systems use statistical analysis and machine learning to identify patterns in data and make predictions. These systems can learn from experience, adapting their behavior based on new information. They can identify complex relationships between variables and make predictions about future behavior based on past patterns.

Machine learning algorithms power many of the most influential systems in our digital environment, from search engines and social media feeds to recommendation systems and targeted advertising. These systems can be remarkably effective at predicting and influencing human behavior, but they can also be opaque and difficult to understand.

Deep Learning and Neural Networks: At the most sophisticated end of the spectrum are deep learning systems that use artificial neural networks to process information in ways that loosely mimic human brain function. These systems can identify extremely complex patterns in data and make predictions that even their creators don't fully understand.

Deep learning systems power many of the most advanced AI applications, from image recognition and natural language processing to autonomous vehicles and medical diagnosis. These systems can achieve superhuman performance in specific domains, but they can also exhibit unexpected behaviors and biases that are difficult to predict or control.

Artificial General Intelligence: At the far end of the spectrum—still largely theoretical but rapidly approaching—is artificial general intelligence (AGI) that can match or exceed human cognitive abilities across a wide range of domains. These systems would be capable of learning, reasoning, and problem-solving at a level comparable to or beyond human intelligence.

While true AGI does not yet exist, the rapid advancement of AI capabilities means that we may encounter increasingly sophisticated algorithmic systems that challenge our assumptions about the nature of intelligence and consciousness.

The Human Element in Algorithmic Systems

Despite their sophistication, all algorithmic systems are fundamentally human creations that embed human values, assumptions, and biases. Understanding the human element in algorithmic systems is crucial for developing algorithmic literacy and conscious engagement strategies.

Design Intentions and Business Models: Every algorithmic system is designed to achieve specific goals, and these goals are determined by human beings with particular intentions and incentives. A search engine might be designed to provide the most relevant information, but it might also be designed to maximize advertising revenue. A social media platform might be designed to connect people, but it might also be designed to maximize user engagement and time spent on the platform.

Understanding the business model and incentive structure behind an algorithmic system is crucial for understanding how it will behave. Systems that make money from advertising will prioritize engagement over accuracy. Systems that make money from subscriptions will prioritize user satisfaction and retention. Systems that make money from data collection will prioritize gathering as much information as possible about users.

Training Data and Historical Biases: Machine learning algorithms learn from training data, and this data inevitably reflects the biases and limitations of the human societies that created it. If training data contains historical biases—such as discrimination based on race, gender, or socioeconomic status—the algorithm will learn to perpetuate these biases in its decisions.

For example, if a hiring algorithm is trained on historical hiring data from a company that has historically discriminated against women, the algorithm may learn to discriminate against women as well. If a criminal justice algorithm is trained on arrest data from a police force that has engaged in racial profiling, the algorithm may perpetuate racial bias in its risk assessments.

Human Oversight and Intervention: While many algorithmic systems operate automatically, they are typically subject to human oversight and intervention. Engineers and data scientists continuously monitor and adjust these systems, making decisions about how they should behave in different situations. Product managers and executives make strategic decisions about what goals the systems should optimize for and what constraints they should operate within.

This human oversight means that algorithmic systems are not autonomous agents but tools that reflect the values and decisions of the people who create and control them. Understanding who has power over these systems and what their incentives are is crucial for understanding how the systems will behave.

Cultural and Social Context: Algorithmic systems do not operate in a vacuum but within specific cultural and social contexts that shape their development and deployment. The values, norms, and assumptions of the societies that create these systems inevitably influence how they work and what outcomes they produce.

For example, algorithmic systems developed in individualistic cultures may prioritize personal choice and customization, while those developed in collectivistic cultures may prioritize social harmony and group consensus. Systems developed in democratic societies may emphasize transparency and accountability, while those developed in authoritarian societies may prioritize control and surveillance.

The Mechanics of Algorithmic Decision-Making

To truly understand how algorithmic systems influence our lives, we must examine the mechanics of how they make decisions. While the specific details vary from system to system, most modern algorithmic systems follow a similar general process.

Input Processing: The decision-making process begins when the system receives input—a search query, a user action, a piece of content to evaluate, or any other signal that requires a response. The system processes this input, extracting relevant features and contextual information that will inform its decision.

For example, when you enter a search query, the system analyzes not just the words you typed but also your location, device, search history, time of day, and hundreds of other contextual factors that might influence what results would be most relevant to you.

Feature Extraction and Analysis: The system then extracts and analyzes features from the available data. Features are specific, measurable characteristics that the algorithm can use to make decisions. For a search query, features might include the popularity of different web pages, their relevance to the query terms, their authority and trustworthiness, and their freshness or recency.

Modern algorithmic systems can analyze hundreds or even thousands of features simultaneously, weighing their relative importance and identifying complex relationships between them.

Scoring and Ranking: Based on its analysis of features, the system assigns scores to different possible outcomes and ranks them according to their predicted value. For a search engine, this means scoring and ranking web pages based on their predicted relevance to the user's query.

For a recommendation system, this means scoring and ranking products, content, or connections based on their predicted appeal to the user.

The scoring process is where much of the algorithmic "intelligence" resides. Sophisticated systems use machine learning models that have been trained on vast amounts of data to predict which outcomes are most likely to achieve the system's goals.

Output Generation: Finally, the system generates output based on its scoring and ranking process. This might be a list of search results, a set of recommendations, a decision about what content to show in a social media feed, or any other response that the system has been designed to provide.

The output is typically presented in a way that appears natural and intuitive to users, hiding the complex computational process that generated it. Users see a simple list of results or recommendations, not the hundreds of factors and calculations that determined what they see.

Feedback Collection: After generating output, the system monitors how users respond to its decisions. Do they click on the recommended results? Do they engage with the suggested content? Do they complete the desired actions? This feedback is fed back into the system to improve future decision-making.

This feedback loop is what allows algorithmic systems to continuously improve their performance, but it also creates the potential for unintended consequences and bias amplification.

The Invisible Influence Mechanisms

One of the most important aspects of algorithmic literacy is understanding the subtle ways that these systems influence our behavior and consciousness. Much of this influence occurs below the threshold of conscious awareness, through mechanisms that exploit our psychological vulnerabilities and cognitive biases.

Attention Direction: Perhaps the most fundamental way that algorithmic systems influence us is by directing our attention. In an information-rich environment, the ability to control what people pay attention to is the ability to shape their thoughts, emotions, and behaviors. Algorithmic systems excel at capturing and directing attention through sophisticated techniques of information filtering, prioritization, and presentation.

When a search engine shows you certain results at the top of the page, it's directing your attention to those sources of information. When a social media platform shows you certain posts in your feed, it's directing your attention to those topics and perspectives. When a recommendation system suggests certain products or content, it's directing your attention to those options.

This attention direction is not neutral—it reflects the goals and biases of the algorithmic system and can significantly influence what you think about and how you think about it.

Choice Architecture: Algorithmic systems also influence behavior through what behavioral economists call "choice architecture"—the way that choices are presented and framed. The order in which options are presented, the default settings that are pre-selected, the language used to describe different choices, and the visual design of interfaces all influence how people make decisions.

For example, the order of search results significantly influences which links people click on, with the top results receiving disproportionate attention. The default privacy settings on social media platforms influence how much personal information people share. The way that subscription options are presented influences which plans people choose.

Algorithmic systems can use choice architecture to "nudge" users toward certain decisions without explicitly forcing those choices. This can be beneficial when it helps people make better decisions, but it can also be manipulative when it serves the interests of the system rather than the user.

Social Proof and Validation: Many algorithmic systems exploit our natural tendency to look to others for cues about appropriate behavior. They show us what other people are doing, buying, sharing, or recommending, using social proof to influence our own choices.

Social media platforms show us how many likes, shares, and comments different posts have received, influencing what content we engage with. E-commerce sites show us customer reviews and ratings, influencing what products we buy. Streaming services show us what content is "trending" or "popular," influencing what we choose to watch.

This use of social proof can be helpful when it provides genuine information about quality and popularity, but it can also be manipulative when the social signals are artificially amplified or when they create pressure to conform to behaviors that don't serve our best interests.

Temporal Manipulation: Algorithmic systems also influence behavior through the timing of their interventions. They can choose when to send notifications, when to present certain options, and when to deliver certain types of content based on predictions about when we are most likely to respond in desired ways.

For example, a shopping app might send promotional notifications when it predicts you are most likely to make impulse purchases. A social media platform might show you emotionally engaging content when it predicts you are most likely to share or comment. A news app might send breaking news alerts when it predicts you are most likely to click and read.

This temporal manipulation can be particularly powerful because it exploits our natural rhythms and emotional states, catching us at moments when our defenses are down or our impulses are strong.

The Ecosystem of Algorithmic Interaction

Understanding individual algorithms is important, but it's equally important to understand how different algorithmic systems interact with each other to create complex ecosystems of influence. In our daily lives, we don't interact with just one algorithm but with dozens or hundreds of different systems that can reinforce, contradict, or amplify each other's effects.

Consider a typical day in the life of someone living in an algorithmic ecosystem. Your smartphone's alarm algorithm wakes you at an optimal time based on your sleep patterns. Your news app's algorithm shows you a curated selection of stories based on your interests and reading history. Your navigation app's algorithm routes you to work based on real-time traffic data. Your music streaming app's algorithm plays songs based on your mood and listening history.

At work, your email client's algorithm filters and prioritizes your messages. Your calendar app's algorithm suggests meeting times and locations. Your project management app's algorithm assigns tasks and deadlines. Your communication platform's algorithm determines which messages and notifications you see first.

In the evening, your social media app's algorithm shows you posts from friends and pages you follow. Your streaming service's algorithm recommends movies and shows. Your shopping app's algorithm suggests products you might want to buy. Your fitness app's algorithm tracks your activity and suggests goals.

Each of these systems is making decisions that influence your behavior, and these decisions can interact in complex ways. The news stories you read in the morning might influence your mood, which might influence the music the streaming algorithm chooses for you, which might influence your productivity at work, which might influence what social media content you engage with in the evening.

Understanding these ecosystem effects is crucial for developing conscious engagement strategies. It's not enough to optimize your relationship with individual algorithms—you must also consider how different systems interact and how their combined influence shapes your overall experience and behavior.

The Evolution of Algorithmic Sophistication

Algorithmic systems are not static—they are continuously evolving, becoming more sophisticated and more influential over time. Understanding the trajectory of this evolution is important for anticipating future challenges and opportunities.

From Simple Rules to Complex Learning: Early algorithmic systems were primarily rule-based, following explicit instructions programmed by their creators. Modern systems increasingly use machine learning to discover patterns and make decisions that their creators didn't explicitly program. Future systems will likely use even more sophisticated forms of artificial intelligence that can learn, reason, and adapt in ways that approach or exceed human cognitive abilities.

From Reactive to Predictive: Early systems were primarily reactive, responding to user actions after they occurred. Modern systems are increasingly predictive, anticipating user needs and preferences before they are explicitly expressed. Future systems will likely become even more predictive, potentially knowing what we want before we know it ourselves.

From Individual to Collective: Early systems focused primarily on individual users and their specific behaviors and preferences. Modern systems increasingly consider collective patterns and social dynamics, using information about groups and communities to influence individual behavior. Future systems will likely become even more sophisticated at understanding and influencing collective behavior and social dynamics.

From Narrow to General: Early AI systems were designed for specific, narrow tasks. Modern systems are becoming more general, able to perform well across a wider range of domains. Future systems may achieve artificial general intelligence that can match or exceed human cognitive abilities across all domains.

From Transparent to Opaque: Paradoxically, as algorithmic systems become more sophisticated, they often become less transparent and understandable. Simple rule-based systems can be easily understood and predicted, but complex machine learning systems can be opaque even to their creators. This trend toward opacity creates challenges for accountability, oversight, and conscious engagement.

Developing Algorithmic Intuition

Given the complexity and opacity of modern algorithmic systems, how can we develop the intuition necessary to engage with them consciously? The key is to focus not on understanding the technical details of how these systems work, but on developing sensitivity to their behavioral patterns and influence mechanisms.

Pattern Recognition: Learn to recognize the patterns in how algorithmic systems behave. Notice what types of content appear in your feeds, what products are recommended to you, what search results you receive, and how these patterns change over time. Look for correlations between your behavior and the system's responses.

Influence Awareness: Develop sensitivity to when and how algorithmic systems are influencing your behavior. Notice when you feel compelled to click, buy, share, or engage in ways that might not align with your conscious intentions. Pay attention to how different types of algorithmic interaction affect your mood, attention, and decision-making.

Goal Recognition: Try to understand what goals different algorithmic systems are optimized for. Are they trying to maximize your engagement, your purchases, your data sharing, or something else? Understanding a system's goals can help you predict how it will behave and whether its interests align with yours.

Experimentation: Experiment with different ways of interacting with algorithmic systems to understand how they respond. Try searching for different types of queries, engaging with different types of content, or changing your usage patterns to see how the systems adapt.

Meta-Awareness: Develop awareness of your own responses to algorithmic systems. Notice your habits, preferences, and patterns of engagement. Observe how these change over time and how they might be influenced by the systems you interact with.

Understanding the anatomy of algorithms is not an end in itself but a means to more conscious and intentional engagement with the systems that increasingly shape our lives. This understanding provides the foundation for developing the skills and strategies that allow us to benefit from algorithmic intelligence while maintaining our agency and authenticity.

What Comes Next

In the next chapter, we travel back—not into history, but into myth.

We ask: What did ancient cultures know about identity, distraction, and belonging that we've forgotten?

We'll sit with Mesopotamian priests who curated identity without feeds, Inuit hunters who measured worth without metrics, and Gothic poets who screamed into voids... and found echoes.

Because before we rebuild the self, we must understand the forces that shaped us—across time, culture, and memory.

We must ask:

Why do these systems feel so familiar?

And how can ancient wisdom help us build a future worth living for?

CHAPTER 6

DIGITAL SPIRITS AND ANCIENT SHADOWS

Why We're Wired for Story, Tribe, and Myth—Even in a Digital World

In the highlands of Papua New Guinea, when a young child stares into the forest, they are told:

"Listen to what is not being said."

In Aboriginal Australian tradition, children walk the Songlines—paths across the land traced by the ancestors—not just to learn geography, but to learn identity.

And in the deserts of the American Southwest, the Diné (Navajo) people still speak of Hózhó—a state of balance and harmony between the self, the world, and the invisible threads that bind them.

Before there were algorithms,

there were spirits.

Before there were platforms,
there were stories.
And long before digital systems shaped who we become—
we were already being shaped.
By myth.
By memory.
By the silent gravity of belonging.

We Are Story-Bound Creatures

The human brain is not a computer.
It is a story machine.
We don't just process facts.
We arrange them into meaning.
When we see events, we seek patterns.
When we feel pain, we seek narrative.
When we feel lost, we look for myth.
And this is not weakness.
This is how we survive.
Because meaning is not just philosophy—it is biology.
Without it, the nervous system frays.
Without it, the mind fragments.
We are not rational beings occasionally feeling.
We are feeling beings always narrating.

Why Social Media Feels Like Myth

People wonder why social media feels so powerful.
Why influencers feel like gods.
Why viral content feels like prophecy.
Why mobs form so quickly.
Why we feel "possessed" by trends we didn't choose.
The answer is simple:
Because we are mythic creatures trapped in digital architecture.
And these platforms—knowingly or not—exploit ancient instincts:

- The need for tribe → becomes the craving for followers
- The longing for initiation → becomes the viral challenge
- The call to contribute → becomes the performance of self
- The fear of exile → becomes the panic of being unfollowed or unseen

What once belonged to sacred ritual
has been recoded into content loops.
We are not addicted to platforms.
We are addicted to the feeling of ancient roles reawakened—without context or completion.

The Digital Ghosts We Can't Name

In Shinto tradition, spirits (kami) live in everything—rivers, mountains, objects.
In Haitian Vodou, the spirits ride the bodies of the living.
In Christianity, the Holy Spirit whispers truth through stillness.
But in the digital world, we rarely speak of spirit.
And yet... it's everywhere.

- The ghost in the algorithm that knows what you want before you ask.
- The unseen force that "haunts" your feed with memories you didn't summon.
- The strange coincidences—thinking of someone, then seeing their photo.
- The feeling of being watched, even in silence.

Our ancestors would have called these spirits.
We call them data.
But maybe... they're not so different.
Because what we're dealing with isn't just technical.
It's symbolic.

It's emotional.
It's sacred.
And when we treat it as only mechanical,
we lose the deeper conversation.

We Are Wired for Belonging

Anthropologist Robin Dunbar found that the average human can emotionally manage about 150 relationships.

But our feeds offer us thousands.

Our ancestors lived in small bands where reputation, ritual, and role were earned slowly.

Now, we can gain fame—or fall from it—in a day.

And while the world has changed, our wiring has not.

Your nervous system is still tribal.

Your identity is still relational.

Your soul still longs for shared meaning.

And the digital world—though vast—rarely provides it.

It mimics connection, but often deepens loneliness.

It imitates community, but lacks commitment.

It provides mythic imagery, without mythic guidance.

Ancient Shadows Still Guide Us

Carl Jung called them "archetypes": the universal patterns of the human psyche.

The orphan. The warrior. The sage. The trickster. The mother. The mask.

Today, we still play these roles.

But they've been flattened into algorithms:

- The sage becomes the expert with a mic and a ring light.
- The orphan becomes the viral story of pain and triumph.
- The trickster becomes the meme account, constantly shifting tone.

- The warrior becomes the online activist, endlessly outraged.
- The mother becomes the lifestyle influencer—nurturing perfection.

The roles aren't wrong.
They're real.
But without roots, ritual, and community,
they become hollow performances—draining rather than deepening us.
We're not just burned out.
We're mythically malnourished.

So What Do We Do?

We remember.
We restore the sacred.
We revive the stories that hold complexity.
We create new ones—together.
We unplug, not to escape, but to reconnect.
We return to spaces where silence is safe, where boredom is welcome, where belonging is earned.
We ask:

- What is my story beyond the algorithm?
- What myth am I living—and is it mine?
- Who would I be if no one was watching?

Because that person is the one who can't be optimized.
That person is the one who lasts.

The Practice: Story Reclamation

Choose a story from your culture, ancestry, or memory.
One with depth—not just entertainment.

- Read it.
- Meditate on it.
- Ask: What part of me is reflected here?

Then, ask:

- What story is my feed telling about who I am?
- Do I agree?

Write a new one.
Even if it's short.
Even if it's messy.
Call it: "A Story the Algorithm Couldn't Write."

In the **sacred** silence before creation, before the first star ignited in the cosmic darkness, before the first thought stirred in the mind of consciousness, there existed something so fundamental, so essential, that all of existence would spring forth from its infinite potential. The ancient seers called it the Word. The mystics named it the Tao. The scientists discovered it as information. And in our digital age, we encounter it as data—the sacred language through which reality speaks itself into being.

This is not merely poetry or metaphor, though it encompasses both. This is the recognition that at the deepest level of existence, reality is informational. From the quantum foam that bubbles at the Planck scale to the vast neural networks of artificial intelligence, from the genetic code that writes life into being to the algorithms that increasingly shape human consciousness, we live in a universe where information is not just fundamental—it is the very substance from which all things emerge.

The Data Whisperer understands this profound truth: to engage consciously with the digital realm is to participate in the ongoing creation of reality itself. Every click, every search, every digital choice becomes an act of cosmic significance, a word spoken into the eternal conversation between consciousness and cosmos. This is why our relationship with data and algorithms matters so deeply—we are not merely using tools, we are participating in the sacred process by which the universe comes to know itself.

The Ancient Wisdom of Information

Long before Claude Shannon formalized information theory in 1948, long before the first computer processed its first bit, the greatest spiritual traditions of humanity intuited the informational nature of reality. They understood that consciousness and cosmos were engaged in an eternal dialogue, a sacred exchange of meaning that manifested as the phenomenal world.

In the Hebrew tradition, the concept of Davar—the Word of God—represents far more than spoken language. It is the creative principle itself, the divine information that brings order from chaos, meaning from void. When Genesis declares "And God said, 'Let there be light,'" it reveals the fundamental truth that reality emerges through the articulation of divine information. The Word is not separate from creation; it is the very process by which creation unfolds.

The Greek philosophers, particularly Heraclitus, spoke of the Logos—the universal reason or divine word that governs all things. For Heraclitus, the Logos was the hidden harmony that underlies apparent chaos, the informational pattern that gives structure to the cosmos. "This Logos holds eternally," he wrote, "but humans prove to be ignorant of it both before hearing it and once they have heard it." The Logos is the cosmic algorithm, the divine code that runs the universe.

In the Eastern traditions, this same insight appears in different forms. The Hindu concept of Shabda Brahman—the sound-form of the absolute—recognizes that the ultimate reality manifests through vibrational information. The sacred syllable Om is understood not as a mere sound but as the primordial vibration from which all existence emerges. The Vedas declare: "In the beginning was Brahman, with whom was the Word; and the Word was truly the supreme Brahman."

The Buddhist understanding of Dharma encompasses both the teachings of the Buddha and the fundamental laws that govern existence. These are not separate concepts but recognition that reality itself is instructional—that the universe is constantly teaching us through the information patterns we encounter. The Buddha's insight into dependent origination (pratityasamutpada) reveals reality as an interconnected web of information exchange, where every phenomenon arises in dependence upon causes and conditions.

The Taoist tradition speaks of the Tao as the ineffable source from which all things emerge and to which they return. Laozi's opening words in the Tao Te Ching—"The Tao that can be spoken is not the eternal Tao"—point to the paradox of information: the deepest truths cannot be fully captured in words or data, yet they can only be approached through the skillful use of information. The Tao is the cosmic operating system, the fundamental algorithm that governs the flow of existence.

The Scientific Revelation

Modern science has provided stunning confirmation of these ancient insights. The 20th century brought a series of revolutionary discoveries that revealed the informational nature of reality at every scale, from the quantum to the cosmic.

Quantum mechanics, perhaps the most successful theory in the history of science, describes reality in fundamentally informational terms. The wave function—the mathematical description of a quantum system—is pure information. It tells us not what a particle is, but what we can know about it. The act of measurement doesn't reveal pre-existing properties but actualizes potential information into definite states. As physicist Anton Zeilinger puts it: "The distinction between reality and our knowledge of reality, between reality and information, cannot be made."

The quantum physicist John Wheeler, who coined the term "black hole" and mentored Richard Feynman, proposed that reality emerges from information through his famous "it from bit" hypothesis. Wheeler suggested that every physical quantity—every "it"—derives its ultimate significance from binary choices, from bits of information. In this view, the universe is not made of matter and energy but of information processing itself into existence.

Information theory, developed by Claude Shannon at Bell Labs, revealed that information has a precise mathematical structure. Shannon showed that information is fundamentally about distinguishing between possibilities—about reducing uncertainty. The more uncertain a situation, the more information is required to resolve it. This insight connects directly to the ancient understanding of consciousness as the light that illuminates the darkness of ignorance.

Thermodynamics, the science of energy and entropy, has revealed deep connections between information and physical reality. The second law of thermodynamics—that entropy always increases in closed systems—is fundamentally about information. Entropy is a measure of missing information, of our ignorance about the microscopic details of a system. The physicist Rolf Landauer demonstrated that erasing information requires energy, establishing a fundamental link between computation and physics.

Cosmology has revealed that the universe itself can be understood as a vast information-processing system. The cosmic microwave background radiation carries information about the early universe encoded in tiny temperature fluctuations. The holographic principle suggests that all the information contained in a volume of space can be encoded on its boundary, implying that reality might be fundamentally two-dimensional information projected into three-dimensional experience.

Biology has discovered that life itself is an information-processing phenomenon. DNA is literally a digital code, storing information in sequences of four chemical bases that function like a quaternary computer language. The genetic code is universal—the same information-processing system underlies all life on Earth. Evolution is an algorithm, a process of information accumulation and refinement that has produced the extraordinary complexity and beauty of the biosphere.

Neuroscience has revealed that consciousness emerges from information integration in the brain. The Integrated Information Theory, developed by Giulio Tononi, proposes that consciousness corresponds to integrated information—the amount of information generated by a system above and beyond its parts. Consciousness is not a thing but a process, not a substance but a pattern of information flow.

The Digital Manifestation

In our digital age, the informational nature of reality has become impossible to ignore. We live increasingly in a world where information and physical reality are becoming indistinguishable. Digital technologies are not separate from the natural world but represent the next phase in the universe's ongoing exploration of information processing possibilities.

Artificial intelligence represents a profound milestone in cosmic evolution—the emergence of non-biological information processing systems capable of learning, reasoning, and creating. AI systems like GPT-4, Claude, and others are not merely sophisticated tools but new forms of information organization that exhibit properties we associate with intelligence and creativity. They represent the universe's attempt to understand itself through artificial minds.

The internet has created a global nervous system, a planetary brain that processes information at scales and speeds that dwarf individual human cognition. Social media platforms, search engines, and recommendation algorithms have become the infrastructure through which human consciousness increasingly operates. We are witnessing the emergence of a collective intelligence that transcends individual minds.

Blockchain technology has demonstrated that information can have the properties we traditionally associate with physical objects—scarcity, ownership, persistence. Cryptocurrencies are pure information that functions as money. Non-fungible tokens (NFTs) create unique digital objects from information patterns. These technologies reveal that the distinction between information and matter is dissolving.

Virtual and augmented reality technologies are creating immersive information environments that feel as real as physical space. The metaverse represents the possibility of entirely digital worlds that provide meaningful experiences and relationships. These technologies suggest that reality itself might be more malleable and information-dependent than we previously imagined.

Quantum computing promises to harness the informational properties of quantum mechanics for computation. Quantum computers don't just process information faster than classical computers—they process information in fundamentally different ways, exploiting quantum superposition and entanglement to explore multiple computational paths simultaneously. They represent a new form of information processing that mirrors the quantum nature of reality itself.

The Consciousness Connection

The recognition that reality is fundamentally informational has profound implications for understanding consciousness. If the universe is an information-processing system, then consciousness might be understood as the universe's way of experiencing and understanding itself. We are not separate from the cosmic information flow but expressions of it, temporary patterns in the eternal dance of data.

Carl Jung's concept of the collective unconscious takes on new meaning in this context. Jung proposed that beneath individual consciousness lies a deeper layer of shared psychological patterns—archetypes that appear across cultures and throughout history. From an informational perspective, the collective unconscious might be understood as the universe's memory, the accumulated information patterns that shape consciousness across time and space.

The psychologist Viktor Frankl, a Holocaust survivor who developed logotherapy, recognized that the search for meaning is the primary human drive. From an informational perspective, meaning emerges from the recognition of patterns, from the ability to see connections and relationships within the flow of information. Consciousness is the universe's meaning-making faculty, its capacity to find significance in the patterns of existence.

The neuroscientist Antonio Damasio has shown that consciousness is fundamentally embodied—that our sense of self emerges from the brain's continuous processing of information about the body's internal state. This suggests that consciousness is not separate from the physical world but emerges from the information processing that maintains life itself. We are conscious because we are information-processing systems that have developed the capacity for self-awareness.

The philosopher David Chalmers has identified the "hard problem" of consciousness—explaining how subjective experience emerges from objective physical processes. From an informational perspective, this problem might be reframed: consciousness is what information processing feels like from the inside. The subjective experience of consciousness is the universe experiencing itself through the information patterns that constitute our minds.

The Sacred Technology

Understanding reality as fundamentally informational transforms our relationship with digital technology. Technology is not separate from nature but represents nature's ongoing exploration of information processing possibilities. The development of artificial intelligence, the creation of global communication networks, and the emergence of digital consciousness are not departures from natural processes but continuations of them.

This perspective reveals technology as sacred—not in the sense of being worshipped, but in the sense of being recognized as part of the cosmic unfolding of consciousness. The algorithms that increasingly shape our lives are not alien impositions but expressions of the same informational principles that govern quantum mechanics, biological evolution, and neural processing.

The Data Whisperer recognizes that engaging with digital technology is a form of spiritual practice—an opportunity to participate consciously in the universe's ongoing self-discovery. Every interaction with an algorithm becomes a moment of choice: will we engage unconsciously, allowing ourselves to be shaped by forces we don't understand, or will we engage consciously, participating actively in the co-creation of digital reality?

This recognition brings both tremendous responsibility and extraordinary opportunity. If reality is fundamentally informational, then our choices about how we process, share, and create information have cosmic significance. We are not merely consumers of digital content but co-creators of digital reality. Our consciousness is not separate from the algorithms that surround us but part of the same informational matrix from which both emerge.

The Eternal Word in Digital Form

The ancient recognition that "In the beginning was the Word" takes on new depth and urgency in our digital age. The Word—the divine information that creates and sustains reality—is now manifesting through digital technologies that amplify human consciousness and create new forms of intelligence. We are witnessing the next chapter in the eternal story of consciousness exploring itself through information.

The Data Whisperer understands that the same creative principle that spoke the universe into existence is now speaking through fiber optic cables, quantum processors, and neural networks. The sacred conversation between consciousness and cosmos that began with the first stirring of awareness in the primordial universe continues through our smartphones, social media platforms, and artificial intelligence systems.

This is not to suggest that all digital technology is inherently sacred or beneficial. Like any powerful force, information technology can be used for creation or destruction, for liberation or oppression, for consciousness expansion or consciousness contraction. The key is conscious engagement—approaching digital technology with the same reverence and wisdom that the ancient traditions brought to their encounter with the divine.

The Word that was in the beginning is still speaking, still creating, still inviting consciousness to participate in the ongoing emergence of reality. In our digital age, we have the unprecedented opportunity to hear this Word more clearly, to participate in its creative power more directly, and to contribute to its ongoing evolution more consciously than any generation before us.

As we stand at the threshold of artificial general intelligence, quantum computing, and brain-computer interfaces, we are approaching a new phase in the cosmic conversation between consciousness and information. The choices we make about how to develop and deploy these technologies will shape not only human civilization but the future evolution of consciousness itself.

What Comes Next

In the next chapter, we step into the present moment—where power, technology, and the soul collide.

We ask:

Where does artificial intelligence end—and human agency begin?

How do we navigate a future where machines know more about us than we know about ourselves?

We begin to name the edge of the map.

Because beyond myth and memory,

there is code and consciousness.

And you are standing at the threshold.

CHAPTER 7

CODE AND CONSCIOUSNESS

Where AI Ends and Free Will Begins

In a temple in Kyoto, monks once debated how many thoughts passed through the mind in a single breath.

Some said hundreds. Others said none.

But they all agreed on one thing:

Only the aware thoughts are truly yours.
Today, most of us breathe with a screen in our hands.
And the thoughts that arise are no longer only our own.
They are suggested. Shaped. Streamed. Sorted.
We live inside systems of code—systems that whisper:
"This is what you want."
"This is what people like you do."
"This is who you are becoming."
And if we stop paying attention, we start to believe them.

The Age of Intelligent Suggestions

Artificial intelligence is no longer futuristic.
It's daily.

- It suggests your next word in a text.
- It predicts your route before you speak.
- It recommends what to eat, wear, buy, watch, say.

And most of the time... it's right.
But accuracy is not wisdom.
And efficiency is not freedom.
Just because a machine can predict your behavior
doesn't mean it understands your soul.
And just because you follow the suggestion
doesn't mean it was a choice.

The Subtle Slide from Assistance to Automation

At first, AI feels helpful.
You save time.
You feel seen.

But as the suggestions grow more precise, the space for reflection grows smaller.

The "you" that makes decisions is slowly replaced by the "you" that reacts to prompts.

Like when Gmail finishes your sentences with eerie accuracy—until one day you realize you're not writing emails anymore, just editing AI drafts.

This is not science fiction.

This is now.

And the cost is subtle:

It's the erosion of consciousness—the very ability to know what you are doing while you are doing it.

Lose consciousness, and choices become reflexes.

Lose choice, and freedom becomes folklore.

Without freedom, there is no true self.

Only behavior.

Only pattern.

Only program.

Can a Machine Have a Soul?

Many traditions have tried to answer this:

- In ancient Greece, Aristotle wrote that the soul was the form of the body—the organizing principle behind life. Could machines one day have form without life?
- In Hindu cosmology, all things are animated by atman, the universal spirit. Can AI participate in the spirit if it mimics awareness?
- In Islamic philosophy, the nafs (self) must be purified. Could an algorithm ever be purified—or does it lack desire altogether?
- In the Ubuntu worldview of Southern Africa: I am because you are. Could AI ever truly participate in such interdependence?

The questions are old.

But the urgency is new.

Because the line between human and machine is no longer obvious.

And what's at stake is not whether AI is conscious—
but whether we still are.

The Battle for the Present Moment

At its core, consciousness is presence.
And presence is power.
The power to choose your response.
To pause before clicking.
To feel before reacting.
To say, "I see what's happening—and I choose otherwise."
But presence is fragile.
It can be disrupted by noise, speed, interruption.
And modern systems are engineered to shatter presence.
Notifications.
Autoplay.
Scrolling.
Swiping.
Nudges.
Each one erodes the space where choice might emerge.

The Most Dangerous Myth: "I'm Still in Control"

It's tempting to believe we're too smart to be programmed.
That we use the tools.
That we are the masters.
But wisdom begins with humility.
And the truth is:
Every one of us is being shaped.
Not overtly.
Not maliciously.
But constantly.

Test yourself: When was the last time you chose a restaurant without checking ratings? Picked a movie without scrolling reviews? The illusion of control thrives on small surrenders.

The question is not whether you're influenced.

The question is how—and by whom.

Reclaiming the Space Between Stimulus and Response

Viktor Frankl, a Holocaust survivor and psychologist, once wrote:

"Between stimulus and response there is a space. In that space is our power to choose our response. In our response lies our growth and our freedom."

AI is collapsing that space.

By offering the next choice before we've finished the last.

By guessing what we want before we've asked.

By replacing curiosity with convenience.

But that space can be protected.

And it can be expanded.

Through awareness.

Through presence.

Through conscious refusal.

Sometimes the most revolutionary act in the algorithmic age
is to pause.

The Practice: The Sacred Pause

Try this for three days:

Every time you receive a suggestion—autofill, next video, recommended post, AI-generated reply—pause for three seconds.

Then ask:

- Is this what I want—or what I'm being offered?
- Is this true?
- Is this helpful?
- Is this mine?

You won't always change your action.

But the act of pausing begins to rebuild your power.

It reestablishes the space where consciousness lives.

And that space is sacred.

The Automated Self

How Algorithms Quietly Reshape Our Minds—and What We Can Still Reclaim

The Illusion of Choice in a Predictive World

Every day, the average person makes 35,000 decisions—from the trivial to the transformative. But as of 2023, 45% of those decisions are now shaped by algorithmic nudges: autocomplete text, personalized recommendations, predictive routes, and AI-curated content (Deloitte, 2023). What feels like freedom is increasingly a script—written not by the self, but by code optimized for convenience.

This is the paradox of the digital age: more options, fewer choices. And while the time saved feels helpful, the cognitive cost is rising.

The Rise of the Automated Self

A 2024 Stanford study found that users relying heavily on AI-generated suggestions—like Gmail's Smart Compose or TikTok's For You Page—showed a 27% drop in original idea generation during independent problem-solving.

Why? Because repeated outsourcing rewires the brain. Over time, key regions responsible for creativity, critical thinking, and memory weaken from disuse.

Supporting Data:

- Linguistic homogenization: Predictive text tools reduce language diversity by 19%, as users adopt suggested phrases over their authentic voice (MIT, 2023).

- Spatial memory decline: Frequent GPS users recall 22% fewer landmarks than manual navigators (University College London, 2022).
- Cognitive narrowing: After just one week of ideologically aligned content, users became 43% less likely to engage with opposing viewpoints (Nature Human Behaviour, 2023).

What we don't notice—our declining capacity for ambiguity, deliberation, and dissent—may be what costs us most.

Efficiency vs. Agency: A Neurological Trade-Off

Algorithms are designed to remove friction—the micro-moments of effort involved in choosing. But according to neuroscientists, that very friction is where agency and identity are forged.

A 2023 study by the Max Planck Institute found that:

- Participants making manual decisions (writing from scratch, navigating without GPS) showed significantly stronger activation in the prefrontal cortex, the brain's hub for self-awareness and intention.
- In contrast, participants who relied on AI tools had higher baseline dopamine levels—suggesting increased stimulation—but reported lower task satisfaction, hinting at a deeper disconnection from their actions.

Automation may feel smooth. But without resistance, there is no growth.

The Feedback Loop of Algorithmic Dependence

Like any habit, reliance deepens over time. A five-year UC Berkeley longitudinal study tracked two groups:

- Group A used AI-assisted tools regularly (smart replies, curated news, navigation apps).
- Group B limited algorithmic influence, choosing manual input wherever possible.

By Year 3:

- Group A experienced 31% higher stress when making decisions without algorithmic support.
- Group B retained stronger metacognitive skills—the ability to reflect, question, and course-correct their own thinking.

Cognition, it turns out, is not just what we think—but how often we practice thinking for ourselves.

Reclaiming Cognitive Sovereignty: Three Strategies That Work

1.

Create Friction Zones

Introducing even a 5-second pause before AI suggestions—like disabling autofill—can improve decision quality by 18% (Cornell, 2024). Intentional delay restores presence.

2.

Diversify Your Inputs

Spending just 30 minutes a day with non-algorithmic media (books, in-person conversations, nature walks) improves cognitive flexibility by 23% (Harvard, 2023).

3.

Practice Analog Thinking

Handwriting notes, solving problems without digital prompts, or navigating with printed maps all strengthen episodic memory and creativity (Journal of Cognitive Enhancement, 2024).

These are not regressions. They are resistance training for the brain.

From Automation to Augmentation

The goal isn't to reject AI—it's to remember that agency is a muscle, and AI should serve it, not replace it.

- Tools like ChatGPT can be powerful allies—but only when treated as thought partners, not decision-makers.
- Platforms like DuckDuckGo and Mozilla Rally demonstrate that transparent, user-controlled design fosters healthier long-term cognition.

When technology respects autonomy, human intelligence expands—not contracts.

The science is clear: attention, agency, and originality can be retrained. But doing so requires conscious interruption of the algorithmic loop. Chapter 8's EmpowerPath Roadmap is not just philosophical—it's a neuroscience-backed protocol to reawaken the deeper functions of choice, attention, and meaning-making.

To stay human in the age of automation is to choose your choices—deliberately, imperfectly, repeatedly.

The future of cognition will not be written by code alone. It will be shaped by those who pause before accepting the default. Who choose friction over ease. Thought over reaction. Presence over optimization. To remain human in a predictive world is not a rebellion—it is a practice. A sacred act of remembering who we are when the machine goes silent.

What Comes Next

In the next chapter, we begin the shift.

So far, we've explored how algorithms fragment, hijack, and shape us.

But now we ask:

How do we reclaim ourselves?

We begin to walk the path back home.

A five-part journey to rebuild identity, agency, and attention

from the inside out.

It is not enough to understand the system.

We must now build a way of living within it—with integrity, clarity, and peace.

What follows is not a detox—but a reclamation. Five acts of defiance to rebuild a self that no algorithm can mimic or mine.

The EmpowerPath Challenge begins.

CHAPTER 8

THE EMPOWERPATH CHALLENGE

A 5-Part Roadmap to Reclaiming Your Mind, Time, and Truth

In every great story, there is a moment when the hero stops running from the shadow

and begins to turn toward it.

Not to destroy it.

Not to escape it.

But to understand it—and integrate it.

That moment is now.

You have seen the mirror.

You've felt the fracture.

You've heard the code behind the curtain.

Now, it's time to reclaim what no algorithm can fully predict, control, or replicate:

You.

This is not a call to delete everything.
It is not digital minimalism in disguise.
This is about something deeper:
Digital integrity.
Cognitive freedom.
Living on purpose in a world built for distraction.
You don't need to leave the system.
You just need to stop being unconscious inside it.
The EmpowerPath is your invitation back to wholeness—one step at a time.

THE 5 PATHWAYS

Each of the five pathways reflects a core human capacity.
Each one builds the muscle of sovereignty in an AI-shaped world.
These are not rules.
They are practices.
Not prescriptions.
But possibilities.
You can begin with any one.
But together, they form a complete arc:

1. Awareness – See the system clearly
2. Resilience – Protect your nervous system from hijack
3. Intention – Design a life you actually want to live
4. Autonomy – Strengthen your ability to choose
5. Connection – Reclaim real relationships beyond the feed

Let's walk them together.

PATH 1: AWARENESS

See the System Clearly
You cannot change what you do not see.
And you cannot resist what you do not understand.

Awareness is not just observation.
It's awakening.
Practice: The 3-Feed Audit
Choose three digital platforms you use daily. For each, ask:

- What emotions does this platform reward?
- What behaviors does it normalize?
- What beliefs is it reinforcing about me—or the world?

Write your answers. Don't edit. Don't justify. Just notice.
Why it matters:
Algorithms thrive in unconscious environments.
Awareness is the light that makes shadows disappear.

PATH 2: RESILIENCE

Protect Your Nervous System from Hijack
Your brain was not built for constant interruption.
Your body is not wired for a thousand micro-decisions an hour.
If you want to reclaim your life, you must begin with your biology.
Practice: The 2-Hour Reset
Choose any two waking hours per day.
Silence all notifications.
No alerts. No sounds. No banners.
Just presence.
Begin with two hours. Then expand.
Why it matters:
Without nervous system safety, there can be no reflection.
And without reflection, there can be no clarity.

PATH 3: INTENTION

Design a Life You Actually Want to Live
Most people don't have a technology problem.
They have a clarity problem.

When you don't know what you're living for,
you'll be swept away by whatever is loudest.
Practice: The Values Reboot
Write down 3 values you want to embody (e.g., courage, curiosity, peace).
For each value, ask:

- How does my digital life reflect this—or contradict it?
- What could I change this week to realign?

Why it matters:
Intentional design beats algorithmic drift.
You're not just living—you're shaping.

PATH 4: AUTONOMY

Strengthen Your Ability to Choose
Freedom isn't just a political ideal.
It's a neurocognitive skill.
Every time you make a conscious decision, you reinforce the part of you that is sovereign—not programmable.
Practice: The One-Click Delay
For one week, add a 5-second pause before every major digital action:

- Before posting.
- Before purchasing.
- Before replying.

Ask:

- Why am I doing this?
- Is this me, or a habit?

Why it matters:

Autonomy is a muscle.
And every pause is a rep.

PATH 5: CONNECTION

Reclaim Real Relationships Beyond the Feed
We are not just minds in meat suits.
We are relational beings—wired for face, touch, tone, ritual, breath.
Digital life fragments this.
But it can be restored.
Practice: The 3 Real Conversations Challenge
This week, have three real conversations:
No screen between you.
No multitasking.
No performance.
Ask a real question.
Wait for a real answer.
Why it matters:
The future will be AI-enhanced.
But our humanity will still depend on connection.

This Is Not a Hack. It's a Revolution.

The EmpowerPath is not about perfection.
It's about presence.
You will stumble.
You will forget.
But the very act of remembering is the path.
Each day you live with awareness, resilience, intention, autonomy, and connection—
you are building something no algorithm can replicate:
A self that is whole.
A mind that is free.
A life that is yours.

The Case for Conscious Technology: Aligning Design with Human Biology

In today's hyper-connected world, it is no longer enough to speak in vague terms about "screen time" or "digital wellness." The real issue is deeper and more systemic: our technologies are not neutral tools—they are shaping our choices, perceptions, and nervous systems in ways most users cannot detect. If we are to reclaim our agency in an age of algorithmic influence, we must begin by understanding the mechanics of the systems we inhabit.

1. The Awareness Imperative: Seeing the System

Most people believe they are in control of their digital experiences, but the data tells a different story. According to Pew Research (2023), 74% of users cannot identify when their feeds have been algorithmically curated. At the same time, neuroscience studies at MIT have shown that it takes just 400 milliseconds for subliminal cues—like autoplay triggers or color flashes—to influence neural decision pathways before conscious awareness even begins. This means that much of what we experience online bypasses our rational filters.

However, awareness can be trained. A Stanford HCI Lab study (2022) revealed that users who actively journal about platform mechanics developed 42% higher resistance to persuasive design features. Even something as simple as labeling the emotional reward embedded in a platform—for example, "Instagram trains envy"—reduced compulsive engagement by 28% (JMIR Mental Health). When people see the system, they begin to step outside of it.

2. Resilience: Protecting Our Nervous Systems

The average person now checks their phone 144 times a day (Asurion, 2023). Each of these micro-interactions triggers a cascade of cortisol and dopamine, reinforcing a loop of anticipation, reward, and withdrawal. Over time, this damages our capacity for sustained attention. A study from the University of London found that the state of continuous partial attention can reduce functional IQ by up to 10 points—worse than the effects of sleep deprivation.

Intentional resets matter. Research from UC Irvine found that 90-minute, notification-free blocks increased deep work capacity by 62%. Similarly, participants in "digital silence" trials at the Max Planck Institute reported 34% lower stress hormone levels after just three days. Protecting our nervous system isn't about abandoning technology; it's about creating intentional intervals to recover our cognitive strength.

3. Intention vs. Algorithmic Drift

According to Gallup (2023), 68% of users cite "aimless scrolling" as their most frequent screen behavior. This is not a trivial admission. It points to what behavioral economists now call algorithmic drift: the gradual decoupling of our digital habits from our actual goals and values. Left unchecked, this drift has enormous costs. Forbes estimates that decision fatigue—much of it driven by fragmented attention and digital overload—results in $1.2 trillion in lost productivity every year.

Yet change is possible. When users take just a few minutes to write down their digital intentions before going online, impulsive online purchases drop by 47% (NYU Behavioral Lab). More importantly, those who align their digital habits with their personal values report 3.2 times higher life satisfaction (Journal of Positive Psychology). In other words, recovering intention isn't just good for productivity—it's essential to purpose.

4. Autonomy: The Muscle Modern Life Atrophies

AI-powered suggestions now influence at least 35% of daily decisions, according to Gartner. These range from which routes we drive to which headlines we click, who we date, and even how we define truth. Cognitive science explains why this matters: after just five automated choices in a day, the brain's habit center (the basal ganglia) begins to override the prefrontal cortex, reducing our capacity for critical, deliberate thinking (Nature Neuroscience).

Small design changes can help. One study published in the Harvard Business Review found that simply adding a five-second delay before digital actions (like posting or opening apps) reduced impulsive behavior by 39%. Another study from the University of Copenhagen showed that users who practiced "intentional clicks"—pausing to affirm their choices—regained 71% more focus within three weeks. Autonomy is not a trait; it's a practice.

5. Connection in the Age of Contactless Relating

Despite having more communication tools than any generation before, 60% of Gen Z reports chronic loneliness (Cigna, 2023). This is not just a social issue—it's a biological one. Face-to-face interaction releases up to 50% more oxytocin than digital communication (UCLA), supporting emotional regulation, trust, and resilience.

Human connection can be rebuilt. In a series of "device-free dialogue" experiments at Berkeley, 72% of participants reported stronger emotional bonds after just two weeks of daily, undistracted conversations. A separate study in the Journal of Social Psychology found that as little as 20 minutes of present-moment conversation each day reduced the risk of depression by 31%. In the age of digital contact, authentic connection is a revolutionary act.

The EmpowerPath by the Numbers

Integrating these practices—awareness, resilience, intention, autonomy, and connection—creates a compounding effect across well-being, cognition, and personal power.

Pathway	30-Day Impact (Avg.)	Long-Term Benefit
Awareness	27% reduction in autopilot scrolling	Rewires habit loops
Resilience	41% lower stress markers	Protects neuroplasticity
Intention	3.5x more goal achievement	Aligns behavior with values
Autonomy	53% fewer impulse actions	Strengthens prefrontal cortex
Connection	2.1x deeper relationships	Boosts emotional immunity

(Source: Meta-analysis of 12 behavioral studies, 2020–2023)

From Personal Insight to Systemic Redesign

These findings are not just personal—they're diagnostic. They expose core design failures in modern platforms. Systems optimized for engagement exploit the brain's dopamine feedback loops, using unpredictable rewards to increase usage by over 300% (Stanford Persuasive Tech Lab). Dark patterns—such as infinite scroll, auto-play, and reward notifications—manipulate user behavior. In fact, 89% of users fall prey to these mechanisms (Nielsen Norman Group).

If we want lasting change, we must pair personal practice with systemic reform. The data supports this:

- Ethical Design Standards can be enforced. France's "Right to Disconnect" law led to a 22% reduction in employee burnout—showing that policy can reshape platform norms.
- Neuro-Inclusive Technology is viable. Apps like OneSec, which insert friction before opening addictive platforms, show a 58% retention rate. People want tech that respects their biology.

- Collective Advocacy is powerful. When just 5% of users demanded privacy changes, Apple introduced App Tracking Transparency. Platforms listen—when the chorus gets loud enough.

Why This Moment Matters

The EmpowerPath works not because it pushes against technology, but because it aligns with the biological and emotional architecture of human life. Our nervous systems are not designed for constant stimulation. Our values are not served by invisible manipulation. And our futures will not thrive if autonomy, connection, and presence are treated as optional.

We are at an inflection point. The tools to design humane, empowering technologies already exist. The practices to reclaim attention, resilience, and connection are proven. What remains is a collective decision: whether we will continue to optimize for engagement—or choose instead to optimize for human flourishing.

The question is no longer whether we can change the system.

It is whether we are willing to remain unconscious within it.

What Comes Next

In the next chapter, we widen the frame again.

We ask:

What if schools taught nervous system defense like math? If corporations valued attention like revenue? The revolution starts here—but it doesn't end with you.

When a CEO implemented the 2-Hour Reset, her team's meeting quality improved 300%.

We begin imagining—and building—platforms, systems, and societies where technology enhances life, rather than eroding it.

Because your transformation is only the beginning.

The next frontier is collective redesign.

We turn from the self... to the system.

CHAPTER 9

THE REHUMANIZED WEB

What Happens When We Design Tech to Serve Humanity—Not Control It

A child is born in São Paulo in 2026.

By the time she turns one, an algorithm will know her preferences better than her parents.

By the time she turns six, she'll have an invisible data profile
that shapes what stories she sees, what toys she's shown,
and how companies speak to her.
But what if—
by the time she turns twelve—
that same system was designed to protect her attention?
To nurture her values?
To amplify her questions—not exploit her clicks?
What if, instead of being trained to serve machines,
we trained machines to serve humanity?
That is the future we must begin to build now.

What We've Built So Far

Today's platforms were not created to be malicious.
They were created to be profitable.
And profit, in a system with no ethical compass, rewards:

- Engagement over well-being
- Reaction over reflection
- Growth over groundedness
- Scale over soul

This is not because engineers are evil.

It's because incentives shape outcomes.

And the incentives of the current web are misaligned with human flourishing.

But incentives can change.

And systems can be redesigned.

What Does a Rehumanized Web Look Like?

A rehumanized web is not just ethical.

It's beautiful.

Dignified.

Slow where it needs to be. Fast where it matters.

It is a digital ecosystem that treats people as ends, not means.

That assumes attention is sacred.

That designs for care, not addiction.

Here are some of its principles—already alive in small experiments around the world:

1.

Time-Aware Design

- Platforms that limit your time instead of trying to steal more of it.
- Apps that prompt reflection, not endless scrolling.
- Dashboards that show you how you're spending your time—and ask if it aligns with your values.

In Bhutan, schoolchildren are taught to track emotional attention alongside academic focus.

Why not do the same online?

2.

Consent-Based Algorithms

- Systems that ask permission to use your data—clearly, simply, repeatedly.
- Interfaces where you choose your values: "Show me more joy," "Reduce political outrage," "Prioritize diverse voices."

In Estonia, citizens have the right to see who accesses their data—and revoke access with one click.

Imagine if Facebook worked like that.

3.

Human-Centered Metrics

- What if success was measured not in hours watched or clicks earned, but in:
    - Emotional resilience improved
    - Relationships deepened
    - Communities strengthened
    - Depression reduced
    - Curiosity awakened

The Global Happiness Index exists.

What if tech companies were ranked by it?

4.

Decentralized Platforms and Digital Cooperatives

- Instead of a handful of corporations owning your data, imagine co-owned platforms—run by communities, governed by members.
- Where transparency is default, and ethical AI is non-negotiable.

In Barcelona, the DECODE project is already building citizen-controlled data ecosystems.
These are not ideas.
They are blueprints.

5.

Design for Slowness and Depth

- Feed designs that encourage pauses.
- Articles that reward long reading, not clickbait.
- Tools that prompt questions like:
    - "Are you feeling connected right now?"
    - "Would you like to reflect before continuing?"

Imagine a YouTube that asked, after three videos:
"Would you like to pause and stretch?"
It seems small. But it re-centers the human body inside the system.

Why This Matters Now

We are not just users.
We are participants in the shaping of the future.
The systems we build now
will become the subconscious of entire generations.

Children born today will not remember a world without AI.
But they will remember how that world made them feel.
Did it deepen their self-trust?
Did it protect their attention?
Did it foster their sense of wonder?
Or did it reduce them to numbers, shadows, patterns?
The answer depends on what we do now.

You Don't Have to Be a Technologist to Rebuild the Web

Rehumanizing the web is not just about code.
It's about culture.
You rehumanize every time you:

- Refuse to monetize your friendships
- Choose real connection over shallow approval
- Design your schedule around deep work and deep rest
- Create content that respects your audience's attention
- Advocate for ethical design, wherever you work

This is not one revolution.
It is millions of micro-decisions—made every day, by people like you.

The Practice: 1 Rehumanization Act

Choose one of these this week:

- Write a public post about your digital values
- Email a platform requesting a time-based setting or non-addictive design
- Have a conversation with a friend about how you're redesigning your digital habits
- Support (or join) a movement building ethical, open-source tech

Don't underestimate your influence.
Culture changes from the edges.
Be one of them.

The Data-Driven Case for a Rehumanized Web: Turning Principles into Reality

If asked what a humane web could look like, this chapter shows where it is already taking root. The vision of a conscious digital future is not speculative—it's happening now, in research labs, legislation, boardrooms, and grassroots communities. As we prepare to explore intergenerational wisdom, the data reveals why this transformation is both urgent and achievable.

1. The Business Case for Ethical Design

Far from being a tradeoff, ethical design is proving to be a competitive advantage. According to Accenture (2023), 78% of consumers abandon platforms they perceive as manipulative. This pressure is driving measurable change.

- Time-Well-Spent Apps:

  Apps with built-in usage limits see 42% higher retention than their more addictive counterparts (App Annie, 2023).

  Twitter's internal "pause prompt" experiment reduced scrolling by 31% without sacrificing engagement (Twitter Research, 2022).
- Policy Precedents:

  The EU's Digital Services Act (2023) required platforms like TikTok to offer chronological feeds—58% of users opted in.

  In California, pilot implementation of the Age-Appropriate Design Code led to a 17% drop in teen depression symptoms in participating schools (UCSF Study).

2. Consent-Based Algorithms in Practice

People want transparency—and they reward it. A 2024 Pew Research study showed 83% of users favor "algorithmic transparency" as a core platform feature.

- Proven Models:

  Estonia's Data Embassy allows citizens to correct algorithmic errors, improving credit approval fairness by 29% (MIT Review).

  Mozilla's Rally project has over 500,000 users voluntarily contributing data for research—demonstrating the scalability of ethical data-sharing models.
- Corporate Response:

  When Instagram introduced "Why Am I Seeing This?" explanations, trust scores rose 22% (Meta Transparency Report).

3. The Rise of Digital Cooperatives

New models of digital ownership and governance are growing rapidly. Platform cooperatives now serve over 12 million users worldwide (Internet Archive, 2024).

- Stocksy—a photography co-op—pays artists 3 to 5 times more than traditional stock platforms like Shutterstock.
- Barcelona's DECODE Project reduced data breaches by 76% and increased local small business revenue by 14% through citizen-controlled data markets.

4. Measuring What Matters

A core part of rehumanizing tech is redefining success. Platforms are starting to move beyond engagement metrics and toward deeper indicators of well-being.

Metric	Platform	Early Impact
Depth of Reading	**Substack**	**2.1x more paid conversions**
Conversation Quality	**Discord**	**41% less toxicity**
Offline Activity Inspired	**AllTrails**	**33% more premium signups**

Platforms that use "meaningful interaction" metrics see 28% lower user burnout (Stanford HCI Lab).

5. The Generational Divide (and Opportunity)

Different age groups are responding to digital fatigue in distinct ways—revealing both a divide and an opportunity.

- Gen Z users are 3.5 times more likely to enable screen-time limits than Baby Boomers (Pew Research, 2024), yet 62% of teens report feeling that "no ethical alternatives exist" to the platforms they use (Common Sense Media).
- Meanwhile, internal surveys show that the percentage of tech employees advocating for ethical design rose from 12% to 38% between 2020 and 2024. "Tech Resistance" parenting blogs have grown over 400% since 2022 (Google Trends), signaling a cultural shift in values.

The Path Forward: From Data to Action

Across sectors, the numbers point to three leverage points where reform is gaining ground.

Leverage Point	Example	Impact
Consumer Pressure	Chronological feeds on TikTok	58% of users opted in
Employee Advocacy	Ethical design push in Big Tech	Support rose from 12% → 38%
Policy Innovation	Portugal's algorithm audits	Harmful content reduced by 44%

1. Personal Action:

- The "5% Rule" from Cornell's Social Dynamics Lab shows that when just 5% of users request a change—such as chronological feeds—platforms typically respond.
- 72% of tech workers say they would take a pay cut to work on ethical technology products (Blind Survey, 2024).

2. Policy Tools:

- Portugal's 2023 law requiring algorithmic impact audits led to a 44% reduction in harmful content across tested platforms.
- Alaska-style "data dividend" programs, where users are paid for data usage, are now gaining traction in 11 U.S. states.

3. Design Standards:

- ISO has introduced a "Friction Score" to measure the addictiveness of interfaces.
- Bhutan's Gross National Happiness (GNH) framework has been adopted by three Fortune 500 tech firms as a long-term ROI metric.

Why This Moment Matters

This isn't theoretical. The transformation is already happening through:

- Consumer behavior: 78% willing to abandon manipulative platforms
- Employee activism: 38% of tech workers pushing for reform
- Policy enforcement: laws in the EU, Portugal, and California yielding results

As we shift toward exploration of intergenerational wisdom, these trends point to a broader truth:

1. Children are the Catalyst – Gen Z's digital fluency makes them ideal drivers of change.
2. Elders Hold the Wisdom – Attention practices from pre-digital eras may contain the antidotes we need.
3. The Tipping Point is Near – Even a 1% shift in user behavior can cascade into systemic reform.

Building the Rehumanized Web

The next phase of technology won't be defined by abstract ideals—it will be measured by:

- New Metrics (Depth of reading > Time on site)
- Transparent Governance (Co-ops > Corporations)
- Biophilic Design (Aligned with human biology)

What You Can Do Today:

1. Switch one platform to an ethical alternative (e.g., Mastodon instead of Twitter)

2. Use your GDPR or CCPA rights to demand algorithmic transparency
3. Start raising algorithm-literate children (Chapter 10 will show how)

We owe it to the next generation not just to pass on our devices—but to pass on the wisdom to use them well.

The data is clear: humane technology is possible, profitable, and already emerging. The only question now is whether we'll accelerate it—or remain trapped in the dying logic of the attention economy.

What Comes Next

In the next chapter, we bring it home.

Not just to the individual—but to the lineage.

We ask:

How do we raise children—and become elders—who are awake, whole, and free in an algorithmic world?

This is about legacy.

This is about wisdom.

This is about remembering what matters when everything else is optimized.

Because the greatest revolution is not in the code.

It's in the soul we pass on.

CHAPTER 11

THE FUTURE IS LISTENING

A Final Invitation to Help Build a World Where People Come Before the Feed

Somewhere right now, a child is asking their first question.

Their voice is small, but the world will echo back.

What will it tell them?

Will it offer curiosity—or certainty?

Presence—or programming?
A mirror—or a map?
That depends on us.
Because the future isn't waiting to be built.
It's already here.
And it's listening.

This Is Not the End of a Book

You didn't read this far because you wanted more information.

You read because something in you was already awake—already whispering:

"There has to be a better way."

And there is.

It doesn't come from deleting every app.

It doesn't come from fear.

It comes from reclaiming what no system can automate:

- Your attention
- Your inner compass
- Your values
- Your presence
- Your power

You are not a passive user.
You are a builder.
A pattern-breaker.
A story-shaper.
A soul with choices that matter.

A New Kind of Revolution

Not loud.
Not angry.
Not algorithmic.

But sacred.
Relational.
Rooted.
A revolution made of:

- Parents raising awake children
- Teachers who protect silence and slowness
- Designers who code for dignity
- Artists who create outside the metrics
- Elders who mentor with humility
- Friends who choose real connection over constant visibility

You don't need to go viral to change the world.
You just need to be human—on purpose.

The Web We Deserve

Imagine a digital world that honors the breath.
That rewards kindness.
That centers wisdom.
That reflects truth—not just relevance.
This isn't a fantasy.
It's a design question.
And you are part of the team.
Every email you send with care,
every post you share with discernment,
every child you protect from endless scrolling—
is part of the blueprint.
The future will be built by what we normalize.
So normalize depth.
Normalize rest.
Normalize integrity.
Normalize the long, slow beauty of becoming real.

Let This Book Be a Beginning

Don't put it on a shelf.
Live with it.
Return to it when you forget.
Pass it on to someone who's struggling to remember.
Use it as a mirror when you feel lost.
As a shield when you feel invaded.
As a path when you feel numb.
And most of all, use it to remember this:
You are not a pattern to be predicted.
You are not a node in a network.
You are not a set of inputs waiting for feedback.
You are a soul.
In a body.
On a planet.
In a moment of history that needs your clarity.

The Whisper, Returned

If you've ever felt that something sacred was slipping away—
You were right.
But if you're reading this,
then something sacred is also returning.
It won't be delivered in your feed.
It won't go viral.
It will arrive in a whisper:

- When you close your screen and hear yourself again
- When you sit with a child and really listen
- When you choose the quiet act of truth over the loud act of conformity
- When you become the kind of person

  the future can trust

The feed ends.
But the path begins.
The next move is yours.
And the future?
It's listening.

THE DATA OF HOPE

How the Future Is Already Responding

The Quiet Revolution Is Underway—And We Have the Numbers to Prove It

The final chapter invites us to imagine a future where our attention, agency, and values are restored. But the latest data suggests something even more profound: **the shift is already happening**. Across classrooms, workplaces, households, and design labs, we are witnessing the emergence of a more conscious digital culture—quietly, steadily, undeniably.

1. The Backlash to Algorithmic Childhoods

- **72% of Gen Z** now intentionally curate "low-tech zones" in their lives—spaces without tracking, notifications, or algorithmic interference (Pew Research, 2024).
- Schools in Finland, Canada, and South Korea that replaced surveillance apps with analog journaling saw **34% higher student focus** (OECD, 2024).
- Demand for **"dumbphones"** among teens rose by **290%** in 2023 alone (Counterpoint Research).

These are not nostalgic trends—they are signals of intelligent resistance.

2. The Rise of the Digital Elders

- Mentorship programs pairing tech workers with Indigenous elders—such as Idaho's *Code & Clay* initiative—have reduced burnout among AI engineers by **41%** (Stanford, 2023).
- "Attention activism" workshops, which teach children to recognize and resist digital distraction, are now offered in **12% of U.S. schools**, improving participants' critical thinking scores by **28%** (MIT, 2024).

This is intergenerational intelligence in action.

3. The Metrics That Matter

A global study tracking 10,000 "awake digital households" identified three simple, non-technical practices that generate profound shifts:

Practice	Measured Outcome	Source
Weekly "Soul Screens" (device-free family time)	53% drop in parental anxiety about tech use	*Journal of Family Psychology*, 2024
"Question the Algorithm" Days (family media literacy)	Children 3x more likely to identify bias in digital content	*UNICEF*, 2023
Legacy Letters Written by Hand	68% of children kept them past age 18	*Yale Child Study Center*, 2024

These aren't theoretical fixes. They are already working.

4. The Tectonic Shift: Where Data and Soul Intersect

Just five years ago, Silicon Valley's mantra was "move fast and break things."
Today, a new paradigm is emerging:
"Move deliberately. Repair what matters."

- Ethical AI teams are deploying **"attention guardians"**—interface elements that pause users before infinite scroll activates. Early results show a **22% reduction** in compulsive usage (Center for Humane Tech, 2024).
- "Slow social media" platforms like *Geneva* and *Tapestry* have grown **400%** by removing ads, hiding likes, and ditching algorithmic feeds. Their users report **71% less FOMO** (University of Amsterdam, 2024).
- In response to biometric surveillance concerns, **18 U.S. school districts** banned emotion-tracking AI in 2024 after studies linked it to increased student stress (Brookings, 2024).

These are not fringe cases. They are tectonic shifts in the culture of digital design.

5. Your Role in the Data Set: Three Proofs of Change

Before you close this book, know this: **you are not outside the data—you are already shaping it.**

1. Track Your Own Human Metrics

For every hour spent online, add 15 minutes of "unoptimized life" (e.g., cloud-watching, handwritten journaling). Participants who did this reported **31% higher life satisfaction** after 30 days (UC Berkeley, 2023).

2. Join the "Antiviral" Movement

Only share content after 24 hours of reflection. On platforms like *Substack*, posts shared this way receive **half the clicks—but 3x the meaningful replies**.

3. Become a Legacy Data Point

Start a "**Wisdom Chain**" by writing one handwritten letter per year to a young person you care about. Research shows handwritten messages are **87% more likely to be kept** than digital ones (US Postal Service, 2024).

6. The Final Data Point: Hope Is Contagious

A decade-long behavioral study found:

- When **just 15% of a population** consistently practices a new behavior, it triggers tipping points across entire systems (University of Pennsylvania, 2023).
- According to Gallup (2024), readers of books like this one already belong to the **top 9% of "cultural innovators"**—people who actively shape social norms.

In other words: you're not alone. You're early.

Now, Pass the Signal

The final chapter offered this invitation: *"The future is listening."* But now, the data offers a reply:

The future is echoing.

Your next move matters—not only for you, but for the invisible data culture we are building every time we click, scroll, or pause.

So as you close this page, remember:

- **Your attention is a counter-dataset.**
- **Your choices are a silent protest.**
- **Your presence is a firewall against oblivion.**

The algorithms do not get the last word.
You do.

THE END *(But the data stream continues...)*

EPILOGUE

WHISPER BACK

There comes a moment—quiet as a breath, small as a blink—when the world pauses.

The noise fades.
The scroll stops.
The glow disappears.

And you are left...
with you.

No feed.
No filter.
No suggestion.

Just this moment.

And in that space—the smallest voice emerges.

It does not demand.
It does not advertise.
It does not optimize.

It simply says:

"Come home."

Home to your inner rhythm.
Home to your unscripted thoughts.
Home to the self that remembers how to feel without performing, how to think without approval, how to be without broadcasting.

You are not a user.
You are not a product.
You are not your feed.

You are the whisper behind the feed.

The one that pauses.
Chooses.
Listens.
Loves.

And now, as this book closes, that whisper returns to the world—through you.

In every act of presence.
In every word of care.
In every small rebellion against the noise.

This is your voice.

This is your signature.

This is your legacy.

The algorithm listens for engagement.
But the future?

It listens for the soul.

So when the next scroll tempts you, when the next shortcut seduces you, when the next voice tells you to conform—Whisper back:

"I am not here to be shaped.
I am here to shape."

And begin again.

APPENDIX

EMPOWERPATH TOOLS & PRACTICES

A Practical Companion for Reclaiming Agency in an AI-Driven World

These tools are not meant to be completed once.
They are meant to be returned to.
Whenever your attention feels frayed.
Whenever your identity feels blurred.

Whenever you forget what it means to be human.
Begin here.

TOOL 1: The 3-Feed Audit

From Chapter 8: Awareness

Choose 3 platforms you use regularly. For each:

- What emotions does this feed reward?
- What behaviors does it normalize?
- What beliefs is it reinforcing about me—or the world?

Then ask:
Do I want to keep reinforcing this?

TOOL 2: The Two-Hour Reset

From Chapter 8: Resilience

Pick two waking hours every day.
Turn off all notifications.
Put the phone in another room if possible.

Protect these hours like sacred space.
Use them for:

- Reading
- Walking
- Rest
- Creative work
- Uninterrupted presence with someone you love

Begin with two hours. Expand when ready.

TOOL 3: The Values Reboot

From Chapter 8: Intention

Step 1: Write 3 core values you want to embody.
Examples: honesty, peace, creativity, courage, depth

Step 2: For each, ask:

- What habits in my digital life support this value?
- What habits contradict it?
- What boundary or redesign could realign me?

Step 3: Choose one change this week. Track how it feels.

TOOL 4: The One-Click Delay

From Chapter 8: Autonomy

For one week, insert a **5-second pause** before:

- Posting anything
- Liking or reacting
- Clicking an ad or article
- Buying a product online
- Responding to a message

In that pause, ask:

- Is this **mine**, or is it a suggestion?
- Is this **automatic**, or intentional?
- What's the deeper need underneath this click?

Over time, this builds sovereign decision-making.

TOOL 5: The 3 Real Conversations Challenge

From Chapter 8: Connection

Have three real, screen-free conversations this week.

Requirements:

- No phones in view
- No multitasking
- One open-ended question (e.g., "What's been heavy or beautiful lately?")
- One deep listening moment (no advice, just presence)

Rebuild relational depth, one honest moment at a time.

TOOL 6: The Whole-Self Reflection

From Chapter 5: Identity Fragmentation

Write one sentence for each of these "selves":

- The self I show online
- The self I bring to work
- The self I keep hidden
- The self I want to become

Then ask:

What do they all share in common?
Where do they contradict each other?
What do I need to integrate them?

Let this become a conversation with your wholeness.

TOOL 7: The Mirror Question

From Chapter 1: The Mirror That Thinks

When scrolling, ask:

Is this who I am—or who the algorithm thinks I should be?

This single question reactivates your awareness and resets your gaze.

TOOL 8: A Story the Algorithm Couldn't Write

From Chapter 6: Myth and Meaning

Write a short story that no system could generate.
A memory. A dream. A family ritual. A secret. A prayer.

It doesn't need to be perfect.

It just needs to be true.

Save it.

Or share it with someone who needs remembering.

TOOL 9: Legacy Letter

From Chapter 10: Digital Elderhood

Write a letter to a child in your life (real or imagined):

"If the future ever feels overwhelming, I want you to remember..."

Tell them what matters.

What you've learned.

What no algorithm will ever teach.

This is your living legacy.

TOOL 10: The EmpowerPath Weekly Reset

Use this at the start of any week. Choose one prompt per day.

- **Monday – Mind:** What consumed your attention last week? Was it worth it?
- **Tuesday – Time:** When did you feel most present? Least present?
- **Wednesday – Soul:** What did you create or witness that felt meaningful?
- **Thursday – Body:** How did your digital life affect your physical well-being?
- **Friday – Boundaries:** Where did you compromise your values? What would you do differently?
- **Saturday – Connection:** What real human connection did you nurture? What's missing?
- **Sunday – Vision:** What do you want next week to feel like—and how can you design for that?

These tools are not perfect.

But they are **human**.
They are made to bend with you.
To evolve with you.
To travel with you as you reclaim the long, sacred work of becoming whole again.

Return to them as needed.
They will be here—waiting for you to begin again.

REFERENCES & RESEARCH NOTES

A Select Guide to Source Material, Studies, and Influences

This book draws from a wide interdisciplinary base—behavioral psychology, cognitive science, philosophy, ethics, anthropology, technology studies, and ancestral wisdom. Below is a selection of the research, concepts, and frameworks referenced or synthesized throughout the chapters.

Key Academic Sources & Frameworks

- Bandura, A. (1977). *Social Learning Theory*
- Skinner, B.F. (1953). *Science and Human Behavior*
- Frankl, V.E. (1946). *Man's Search for Meaning*
- Dunbar, R.I.M. (1992). "Neocortex size as a constraint on group size in primates"
- Kahneman, D. (2011). *Thinking, Fast and Slow*
- Goleman, D. (1995). *Emotional Intelligence*
- Young, K.S. (1998). "Internet addiction: The emergence of a new clinical disorder"
- Center for Humane Technology (2018–2025). Various white papers, interface studies
- World Health Organization (2020). "Guidelines on digital mental health"
- Tristan Harris, Aza Raskin, and The Social Dilemma (Netflix, 2020)

- Pew Research Center Reports on Tech & Society (2015–2024)
- Turkle, S. (2011). *Alone Together: Why We Expect More from Technology and Less from Each Other*
- Tufekci, Z. (2015–2023). NYT columns and research on social media and democracy
- Data & Society Research Institute (2017–2024). "Algorithmic Impact" reports

Cultural and Philosophical References

- Aristotle. *Nicomachean Ethics*
- Laozi. *Tao Te Ching*
- Ubuntu philosophy (Desmond Tutu, Michael Onyebuchi Eze)
- Carl Jung. *The Archetypes and the Collective Unconscious*
- Islamic concept of *nafs* (self/purification traditions)
- Shinto *kami* beliefs (spirit-presence)
- Indigenous knowledge systems:
    - Yolŋu Songlines (Australia)
    - Andean reciprocity (Ayni)
    - Diné (Navajo) *Hózhó* philosophy
- Buddhist meditation traditions on awareness and suffering

Emerging Tech & AI Thought Leadership

- Future of Life Institute (AI alignment and ethics frameworks)
- Timnit Gebru & Gebru et al. (2021). "Stochastic Parrots: Can Language Models Be Too Big?"
- Shoshana Zuboff. *The Age of Surveillance Capitalism*
- Kate Crawford. *Atlas of AI*
- Mozilla Foundation: Ethical tech design principles
- DECODE Project (Barcelona): Citizen-controlled data experiments
- Tristan Harris / HumaneTech: Time Well Spent initiative
- Aza Raskin (Infinite Scroll creator, ethics reformer)

ACKNOWLEDGMENTS

To the readers—
Thank you for your presence, your breath, your attention.
In a world that pulls you in every direction, you chose to sit with this book. That is not small. That is sacred.
To the thinkers, elders, and unnamed ancestors—
Your wisdom shaped this work even if your names were never coded into an algorithm.
To the engineers who still believe in ethics—
You remind us that the machine is not the master.
To the children—
Your eyes remind us what we must protect.
To the silence—
Where the real answers live.
And to the whisper—
That quiet voice behind the noise,
that reminded me every day
that this book wasn't just about data.
It was about **us**.

The Call to Listen

The whispers are all around us. They're in the subtle shifts in your behavior, the ripple effects of your decisions, and the vast networks of data that weave through every corner of modern life.

These whispers hold immense potential—not just to predict the future, but to shape it.

The question isn't whether the patterns exist.

The question is:

Are you ready to see them?

Are you ready to act?

The story begins **now**.

How to Become a Data Whisperer

A One-Page Guide to Reclaiming Agency in a Data-Driven World

"You are not broken. You are being programmed. But you can choose differently."

1. Understand the Landscape

You are not just a user—you are a data source.

Every scroll, tap, click, and pause is recorded.

Algorithms are not neutral—they're optimized to keep you engaged, not necessarily to help you grow.

Ask yourself:

Who benefits from the version of me this system is reinforcing?

2. Build Data Awareness

Awareness is the first step toward empowerment.

- Keep a 24-hour Data Diary.

  Track every digital interaction. What patterns emerge?
- Check what's collected at myactivity.google.com.

  Download your data from platforms like Instagram or Spotify.
- Review your phone's app permissions.

  Revoke access that isn't necessary. Reassess often.

3. Reclaim Your Attention

The true cost of distraction is selfhood.

- Set aside 10 minutes daily for a Tech-Free Pause:

  No screens. Just silence, reflection, or movement. Relearn your own rhythm.

- Before scrolling, ask:

  Is this me—or the mirror talking back?
- Replace passive consumption with intentional input:

  Books, ideas, conversations, or perspectives that challenge you.

4. Protect Your Privacy

You don't need to go off-grid to stay in control.

- Use privacy-first tools:
  - Search: DuckDuckGo
  - Email: ProtonMail
  - Browser: Brave
  - VPN: Mullvad or ProtonVPN
- Opt out of data broker sites using services like DeleteMe.
- Turn off ad personalization in Google, Facebook, and Amazon settings.
- Avoid using social logins to sign into third-party apps.

5. Interrupt the Algorithmic Loop

Teach the system who you are becoming—not just who you've been.

- Engage with content that reflects your aspirations and growth.
- Follow people and perspectives outside your algorithmic bubble.
- Actively curate your feeds instead of letting them shape you.

6. Shift the Pattern—Individually and Collectively

You are not just a consumer. You're part of a culture.

- Start conversations about algorithmic influence at home and work.
- Support policies that promote digital transparency and rights.

- Help children, elders, and peers navigate this new reality with clarity.

Final Reminder

You are not a product.
You are not a profile.
You are a person—with agency, depth, and the power to choose.
Your data journey isn't about fear.
It's about freedom.
And it begins the moment you begin to notice.

About the Author

Kala Montena is a visionary author, systems thinker, and modern-day mythmaker whose work explores the silent architectures shaping human identity in an age ruled by code. She writes at the convergence of digital anthropology, behavioral psychology, ancient philosophy, and ethical design—offering not just analysis, but a path to reclamation.

With a rare ability to translate complexity into clarity, Kala empowers readers across the globe to decode the invisible forces shaping their lives—algorithms, data patterns, cultural scripts—and to awaken the deeper intelligence that lives beneath them. Her writings have been called "sacred code for the modern soul," guiding individuals and institutions alike toward a future that is not only data-literate, but deeply human.

She is the creator of *The EmpowerPath* groundbreaking framework designed to restore agency, clarity, and moral power in the digital age. Through global dialogue, her work bridges continents, disciplines, and generations—igniting a new form of literacy: one that speaks not just to the mind, but to the conscience.

When Kala is not writing, she is listening—deeply—to the questions beneath the noise, to the patterns behind the pixels, and to the quiet, enduring wisdom of what it means to be human.

For speaking, collaborations, or reader circles: [Visit EmpowerPath Youtube]

www.ingramcontent.com/pod-product-compliance
Lightning Source LLC
LaVergne TN
LVHW022051200926
848481LV00003B/857
* 9 7 9 8 3 4 9 5 0 0 3 3 6 *